C000241848

TEACHING THE HOLOCAUST IN
SCHOOL HISTORY

Also available from Continuum

Philosophy of Education − Richard Pring
Theory of Education − David Turner
Analysing Underachievement in Schools − Emma Smith
Education and Community − Dianne Gereluk
Perspectives of Quality in Adult Learning − Peter Boshier
Private Education − Geoffrey Walford
Pedagogy and the University − Monica McLean
Markets and Equity in Education − Geoffrey Walford

TEACHING THE HOLOCAUST IN SCHOOL HISTORY

Teachers or Preachers?

LUCY RUSSELL

Continuum International Publishing Group
The Tower Building, 11 York Road, London SE1 7NX
80 Maiden Lane, Suite 704, New York, NY 10038

© Lucy Russell 2006

All rights reserved. No part of this publication may be reproduced or transmitted in
any form or by any means, electronic or mechanical, including photocopying, recording,
or any information storage or retrieval system, without prior permission in writing from
the publishers.

Lucy Russell has asserted her right under the Copyright, Designs and Patents Act, 1988,
to be identified as Author of this work.

British Library Cataloguing-in-Publication Data
A catalogue record for this book is available from the British Library.

ISBN: 0-8264-9082-4 (hardback)

Library of Congress Cataloging-in-Publication Data
A catalog record for this book is available from the Library of Congress.

Typeset by Aarontype Limited, Easton, Bristol
Printed and bound in Great Britain by Biddles, Norfolk

If awareness of the importance of individual action and inaction causes students to reflect on their own role in society then all well and good, but while it is our responsibility to support them in this reflection, it is not our right to shape the history in order that they arrive at the same conclusions as ourselves. Otherwise, we cease to be teachers and become preachers. (Salmons, correspondence, 29 September 2005)

Contents

Acknowledgements

This book would not have been written without the support and advice of Clyde Chitty.

I would like to thank all those who gave up their time to be interviewed by me, especially those involved in the development and revision of the National Curriculum for History, and the history teachers interviewed, and John Fox and Paul Salmons.

My grateful thanks to the Office of Public Sector Information for their permission to use History Working Group documentation in this research and the Holocaust Educational Trust for access to their archives.

Thank you to all those at Continuum for their work on this project.

I am also grateful for the support I have received from my family. My husband, Glyn, and my parents have read countless drafts. This book is dedicated to them, to James Gabriel, and to Michael, Margaret and Katherine-Anne.

Abbreviations

BBC	British Broadcasting Corporation
BNP	British National Party
DES	Department of Education and Science
DfE	Department for Education
DfES	Department for Education and Skills
ERA	Education Reform Act
GCSE	General Certificate of Secondary Education
HET	Holocaust Educational Trust
HMI	Her Majesty's Inspectorate or Her Majesty's Inspector
HSU	History Study Unit
HWG	History Working Group
ICT	Information and Communications Technology
ILEA	Inner London Education Authority
LEA	Local Education Authority
MP	Member of Parliament
NC/HWG	National Curriculum History Working Group Minutes
NCVQ	National Council for Vocational Qualifications
Ofsted	Office for Standards in Education
PGCE	Post-Graduate Certificate in Education
PSHE	Personal Social and Health Education
QC	Queen's Council
QCA	Qualifications and Curriculum Authority
RE	Religious Education
SCAA	Schools Curriculum and Assessment Authority
SEAC	Schools Examinations and Assessment Council
SHP	Schools History Project
TES	*Times Educational Supplement*
THES	*Times Higher Education Supplement*
UN	United Nations

Chronology of the topic of the Holocaust in the National Curriculum

This time line is set against a backdrop of national and international events from which curriculum developments cannot be seen in complete isolation.

1987
An All Party Parliamentary War Crimes Group is set up to look into allegations concerning Nazi war criminals and to make suggestions regarding possible legislation. The 1991 War Crimes Act will be the result.

1988
25 January
The first meeting of the Holocaust Educational Trust (HET) takes place in the House of Commons. Labour Member of Parliament (MP) Greville (now Lord) Janner is Chairperson of this newly formed trust.

29 March
An article appears in the *Jewish Chronicle* reporting on plans to develop a General Certificate of Secondary Education (GCSE) textbook on the Holocaust. Carrie Supple, a Jewish history teacher from Newcastle is researching and writing the book which will be designed for cross-curricular use.

22 April
Robert Kilroy-Silk writes a piece for *The Times* criticizing the education system which he says fails to teach young people about the Holocaust.

1989
24 January
The History Working Group (HWG) meets for the first time at Elizabeth House in London. Kenneth Baker (the Secretary of State for Education) visits the Group.

17 April

One HWG member faxes a list of topics for consideration to Jenny Worsfold (HWG Secretary). The HWG have deliberately left it until late April to discuss curriculum content, aware that this would be a contentious issue and concerned to get the attainment targets in place first.

29 May

Dr John Roberts writes to Commdr. Saunders Watson of his intention to resign from the HWG at the end of June following the completion of the interim report. He feels unable to balance his commitments as Warden of Merton College, Oxford and a high-profile academic historian with sitting on the Group.

30 May–1 June

The HWG meets at Hebden Bridge. The first draft of the interim report is produced. The decision is made that the topic of the Second World War and the Nazis will not be included as a compulsory study unit in its own right.

3 June

China: students are killed in the Tiananmen Square massacre.

7–10 June

The HWG meet at Elizabeth House and look at the draft interim report. 'Britain in the twentieth century' is the only exemplar programme of study included in the report. No reference is made in this exemplar to the events of the Second World War.

16 June

A paper is written by one group member about overload at Key Stage 4 proposing the trimming of 'Modern Britain', compensated by a linking unit on the Second World War, including the Nazis and the Holocaust instead of China.

24 July

John MacGregor replaces Kenneth Baker as Secretary of State for Education.

25 July

The HWG meets at Elizabeth House. The Chairperson reports that Baker and Angela Rumbold (Education Minister) 'were generally pleased with the [interim] Report. They had a couple of niggling doubts, first about knowledge being in the Programmes of Study rather than the attainment targets, and secondly about there being insufficient emphasis on British history' (NC/HWG (89) 12th).

Professor Peter Marshall has now replaced John Roberts.

10 August
The interim report is published.

30 August–1 September
The HWG meets. The Chairperson had now met with John MacGregor who was concerned about chronology, the proportion of British history in Key Stage 3 and 4 and historical knowledge and its assessment.

The Chairperson announces the setting up of three panels to deal with the tasks ahead:

1. Programmes of Study Panel: Alice Prochaska (convener), Peter Marshall and Peter Livsey.
2. Responses Panel: Jim Hendy (convener), Tom Hobhouse and Robert Guyver.
3. Assessment Panel: Carol White (convener), Ann Low-Beer, Gareth Elwyn Jones and Tim Lomas.

1 September
An article appears in the *TES*, 'Whose Myth is it Anyway?' bewailing the omission of Britain in the Second World War from the interim report.

3 September
Fiftieth anniversary of the outbreak of the Second World War.

5 September
Colloquy of historians meet at Chatham House, London to discuss the National Curriculum for History.

8 September
An article appears in the *Jewish Chronicle* under the headline 'Don't Drop Holocaust' reporting that the HET will campaign for a key place on the school curriculum for the Second World War following the 'outcry over the exclusion of the war in a list of compulsory subjects recommended for a new National Curriculum'.

9 September
A study unit 'World at War 1939–45' is proposed for Key Stage 4 by a group member who attended the colloquy of historians.

26 September

The member of the Programmes of Study Panel who has been working on a draft of the programmes of study sees difficulty in teaching about 1939 without going back to at least 1933. The unit is changed to '1933–45: Second World War, advent, course and aftermath'.

29 September

The HWG meets at Elizabeth House. The responses panel give an interim report summarizing the nature of the responses received so far. Comments include the omission of the Second World War and the Nazis, the Reformation and 'Medicine through Time'.

The Group accepts the proposals from the Programmes of Study panel which include a new study unit, 'The Second World War: its advent, course and aftermath, 1933–1948'.

A cross-party group of MPs (Greville Janner, John Marshall, Robert Rhodes James and Jeff Rooker) send a submission on the teaching of the Second World War and the rise and fall of Nazi Germany to John MacGregor and the HWG. They criticize the omission of the rise of fascism and the Holocaust.

Also this month, *Teaching the Holocaust: the report of a survey in the United Kingdom* (Fox 1989) is published.

2 October

A story in *The Times* under the headline 'MPs Denounce Omissions' reports on the submission from the cross-party group of MPs. The piece concludes, 'the MPs believe few schools would choose to study the War.'

6 October

The *Jewish Chronicle* reports on the submission from the cross-party group of MPs.

9–11 October

The 15th meeting of the HWG. It is reported that responses received about Key Stage 4 include comments that there was too much 20th-century history and the Second World War and Nazi Germany should be included.

11 October

John MacGregor writes in reply to the group of MPs reminding them that the interim report sets out the Group's initial thinking and that opportunities exist within their current proposals for the inclusion of the Second World War and the Nazis in the school curriculum.

13 October
An article appears in the *TES*, 'Critics Force History Group to Rewrite Report'. This article refers to the submission from the all-party group of MPs. It is also reported that the Historical Association will, on this day, submit detailed comments to the HWG, including the neglect of 1929–45 and the rise of totalitarianism. Martin Roberts, Chairperson of the Historical Association Education Committee is quoted, 'if you don't cover that part of the twentieth century crucial aspects of the modern world cannot be understood'.

20 October
HWG meet for the 16th time. A member of the Responses Panel reads the paper he has prepared summarizing the responses received to date. He notes that the Top 3 most commonly mentioned omissions are:

1. The Holocaust
2. The rise of fascism and the rise of Nazi Germany
3. The First and Second World Wars (both the British Legion and the Western Front Association wrote about this) (NC/HWG (89) 16th).

He also notes, 'secondary teachers' perceptions of omissions coincided generally with the perceptions of the wider public response (e.g., WWI, WWII; more European history, etc). Though the omission of the "history of medicine" was remarked upon mainly by teachers' (NC/HWG (89) 16th).

2 November
MacGregor leaves Education and is replaced by Kenneth Clarke.

9 November
Germany: the Berlin Wall is opened.

14 November
The HWG are meeting in Great Yarmouth when Angela Rumbold says in the House of Commons that the Second World War and Nazism will be in the final report.

26 November
Clarke announces proposals stating that students can choose to study either history or geography at Key Stage 4 or do a short course in both.

28 November
Margaret Thatcher resigns as Prime Minister.

22 December
Writing in the *Jewish Chronicle*, Lionel Kochan questions the wisdom of teaching the Holocaust to all school students.

1990
January
Final report of the HWG is completed.

11 February
South Africa: Nelson Mandela is released.

27 March
In the House of Commons, Greville Janner asks the Secretary of State for Education and Science when he intends to publish the final report and whether he will make a statement (Hansard, H. of C., Vol. 170, Col 173, 27 March 1990).

April
The first edition of the *HET Bulletin* is published. The article on the front page announces, 'Stop Press: Holocaust Education for Britain's Schools. Children in British schools will soon be learning about the Holocaust as a compulsory part of their curriculum' after 'the number of high level submissions both to the HWG and to Mr MacGregor'.

2 April
In the House of Commons, Janner asks the same question as on March 27 (Hansard, H. of C., Vol. 170, Col 421, 2 April 1990).

3 April
The final report is published. The topic of the Holocaust appears in this report for the first time included as 'Essential Information' under the heading 'Casualties of War' in the study unit 'The Era of the Second World War: 1933 to 1948'. This is one of two compulsory study units recommended for Key Stage 4.

4 April
In the House of Commons, Janner asks the Secretary of State for Education what steps he intends to take to introduce study of the Nazi Holocaust into state schools as a core part of the National Curriculum (Hansard, H. of C., Vol. 170. Col 621, 4 April 1990).

13 April

The *Jewish Chronicle* reports 'Shoah lessons "are essential"'. Janner is quoted, 'as a result of pressure of MPs of all parties and many others, the working party has changed its mind. Having won in principle, it is imperative to make sure that there are adequate resources and time for the subject to be taught effectively'.

28 November

The Institute of Contemporary History and Wiener Library hold a debate 'Teaching the Holocaust: For or Against?' between Professor Lionel Kochan with Dr David Sorkin and Mr Ronnie Landau with Mr Philip Rubenstein.

14 January

The draft orders for history are published.

25 March

The statutory orders for history are published and must be implemented from September. A press release announcing the publication of the final orders for history and geography reiterate that 'the focus of study for 14–16 year olds should be from the turn of the century to about 20 years ago' so as to draw a distinction between history and current affairs. Also, the Secretary of State stated that 'in response to comment that pupils who decided to drop history in the final key stage would do little twentieth century history . . . Key Stage 3 (11–14 year olds) now includes a compulsory study unit on the era of the Second World War' (DES 103/91).

1992
April
John Patten replaces Kenneth Clarke as Secretary of State for Education.

1993
April
Patten announces the Dearing Review. Also this month Bill Clinton opens the Holocaust Memorial Museum in New York.

July
Dearing's interim report is published.

December
Dearing's final report is published confirming history will not be compulsory at Key Stage 4. The National Curriculum is slimmed down. Also this month, *Schindler's List* is released in cinemas in the UK.

1994
May
SCAA publish the draft proposals for history.

July
Gillian Shephard replaces John Patten as Secretary of State for Education.

1995
January
New National Curriculum orders for history are published. Students in Key Stage 3 are to be taught an overview of the 20th century: the First World War and its consequences; the Second World War including the Holocaust and the dropping of the atomic bombs; the legacy of the Second World War for Britain and the world. It is also recommended that students be taught about at least one event, development or personality in depth (DfE 1995: 13).

27 March
Schindler's List education pack sent out to all heads of history in the UK.

1999
Draft orders for history are published following a review of the National Curriculum initiated by the new Labour Government elected in May 1997. The Holocaust is one of only four named historical events which must be taught in Key Stage 3, the other three being the two world wars and the Cold War (DfEE 1999: 22). According to Terry Haydn, under the draft proposals the Holocaust was the '*only* topic specified by name which will be a compulsory part of the History Curriculum' (Haydn 2000: 135, emphasis in the original).

    The DfEE and QCA jointly publish the new orders for history.

2000
6 June
The Holocaust exhibition at the Imperial War Museum in London opens.

2002
September
Citizenship is introduced as a National Curriculum subject, compulsory at Key Stages 3 and 4.

Foreword

Occupying a unique role in the education of young people in England, the Holocaust has featured, with increasing prominence, in the history curriculum for secondary schools since 1991 when the National Curriculum was first introduced. It is currently one of only four named topics which must be taught in history before the end of Key Stage 3 (by which time pupils have reached the age of 14), the other three being the First and Second World Wars and the Cold War.

This important book looks at the often heated debates surrounding the objectives of teaching the Holocaust in school history, both at the level of national policy-making and at that of classroom delivery. The story of the extermination of around 6 million Jews is obviously one that arouses strong emotions, having taken place within living memory in a modern industrialized country in Europe. And there is no doubt that this can also make it difficult to arrive at an easy consensus about its true significance and about the lessons to be learned from it.

Drawing on a wide range of interview data and on an extensive knowledge of existing literature on the subject, Dr Russell shows that the essential rationale behind the privileged status of the Holocaust in the curriculum can be primarily historical, social or moral. It is certainly clear that there was a lack of clarity and consistency at the centre as to the reasons for teaching the Holocaust; and it is argued that this is reflected in the variety of approaches to teaching the topic to be found in the history classroom in secondary schools.

Professor Clyde Chitty
Joint Head of Department of Educational Studies
Goldsmiths College

Preface

History teachers on teaching the Holocaust:

> I want to teach the Holocaust from a moral point of view, not a historical point of view. I play the part in *Schindler's List* where people are going into the gas chambers without any volume but with Enrique Iglesias' 'Hero' playing very, very loudly. I tell pupils just to listen to the words and not to sing along and it's actually quite powerful sort of stuff. I've found it works really well. It gets me every time, I have to turn away. I can't watch it.
> (Marie)

> I probably spend three or four lessons on the Holocaust. The first gives some background and is historical, but the others are from a moral point of view ... Every year I get a couple of girls who cry, and it's not just for effect. They might be Jewish or they are affected by what we've looked at. I do make a big thing of these lessons. I set the scene and I'm very graphic.
> (Hank)

> If you try to remove the morality issue then you are going to get a proper study of history. The morality can come in later when you have all the information in front of you and you've discussed the sources and you have a personal opinion. But to *cloud* the judgement of students, who should be fairly open to that, is very dangerous. We don't teach history in that way for any other topic. And we shouldn't be teaching it that way for the topic of the Holocaust.
> (Anne)

> I feel strongly that History should be taught as an academic enquiry and not in the first instance as a tool in pursuit of other goals. However, it must remain that its teaching is about 'collective memory' and many of the skills learned are transferable into other walks of life. To teach history for political reasons will surely lead to horrors just like the Holocaust, even if those purposes at first sight might seem benign.
> (Harold)

The majority of history teachers interviewed as part of this study taught the Holocaust not as history, but often as something more like Personal Social and Health Education (PSHE) or citizenship. This book asks why this is so and what is the rationale behind teaching the Holocaust in school history. How far should moral issues come into the teaching of the history of the Holocaust? Is it the role of history teachers to teach about values? Or are history teachers in danger of becoming preachers instead of teachers?

Introduction

What is important about teaching the Holocaust in school history?

What should history teachers' objectives be when teaching the Holocaust to students aged 13 and 14? I began to ask myself this question during one lesson I was teaching about the Nuremberg Laws. Students had not grasped what it meant to be Jewish, and I was fielding questions such as 'Why couldn't the Jews convert to another religion?', 'Why didn't they dye their hair blonde?', 'Couldn't they wear coloured contact lenses?' I felt emotionally more involved with the topic of the Holocaust than with other history I taught. What did I want this class to leave the room with? An understanding of what the Nuremberg Laws were? Some empathy with the Jews and a realization that prejudice and racism are wrong? Do we teach the Holocaust to remember the victims? To contextualize the Second World War? To help students to understand that certain social, economic and political situations can give rise to racism and prejudice? To demonstrate the success of democracy over fascism? To debate whether it is right to prosecute war criminals who are now old people? As an antidote to racism and prejudice? As genocide prevention? Which of these objectives should be prioritized by history teachers? There is support and advice for teachers approaching the topic of the Holocaust (for example Davies 2000, Supple 1998). Rather than discussing the difficulties and issues addressed in such literature, 60 years after the liberation of the extermination and concentration camps, this book examines the teaching of the Holocaust in school history in England.

As in 22 states across America, there is, in England, legislation in place mandating the teaching of the Holocaust. The Holocaust has featured, with increasing prominence, in the school history curriculum since 1991 when the National Curriculum was introduced.[1] It is currently one of only four named topics that must be taught in history before the end of Key Stage 3, the other three being the two world wars and the Cold War. In a review of R. J. Evans's *The Coming of the Third Reich*, Neal Ascherson wrote, 'I know that it is untrue to claim that the only bit of history now taught to British school students is the Third Reich. But it is probably true that it is the only bit of history they are almost all taught about' (Ascherson, 30 November 2003).

However, in a BBC poll conducted in 2004 it was found that more than 60 per cent of young people had not heard of Auschwitz.[2] The Holocaust forms a large part of the programmes of study for history, so how can this be? This book provides a possible explanation: the Holocaust is not being taught solely as history, but often as something more like personal, social and health education (PSHE) or citizenship. If the focus of history lessons on the topic of the Holocaust is social and moral, it may explain why young people are sketchy on the historical detail.

Shortly after the National Curriculum became statutory, Reva Klein wrote in the *Times Educational Supplement* (*TES*) that teachers were 'terrified' of teaching the Holocaust (17 April 1992). Many history teachers had not studied or taught the Holocaust before. In the years since, support for teachers has grown: *Lessons of the Holocaust* is a resource pack produced by the Holocaust Educational Trust (HET) and the Spiro Institute; the Imperial War Museum has produced a resource pack, *Reflections*, activities from which can be used as preparation for a visit to the (permanent) Holocaust Exhibition at the Museum; schools can book out a travelling exhibition from the Anne Frank Educational Trust; Holocaust survivors can be booked for classroom visits through the HET; the Imperial War Museum, and the HET, run in-service training on approaches to teaching the Holocaust; and the HET organize visits to Auschwitz for teachers and sixth-form students. However, I struggled to teach about the Holocaust not because I lacked resources but because I was unclear of my objectives. Indeed, the volume of resources (many of which are cross-curricular) did little to help me focus my lessons. A possible 'lack of clarity about the nature of the affective and cognitive aims of such work' was one pedagogical challenge recognized in research about teaching the Holocaust published by Brown and Davies (1998: 80).

It is difficult to separate the cognitive and affective. Carrie Supple argues that the Holocaust must be taught as part of the mainstream syllabus and that its history is important. But the cognitive and the affective are blurred when she writes that the Holocaust:

> is a subject that many teachers may dread tackling due to its complexity and the fact that it seems beyond explanation. How, for example, could human beings dump a truckload of babies into a burning pit and appear to feel nothing? Nonetheless, it is crucial that this history be part of the mainstream syllabus and not sanctified or otherwise made inaccessible. (Supple 1998: 17)

'How could this happen?', or 'What circumstances led human beings to do this?' are cognitive questions; they are historical. But the question 'How could human beings do this and appear to feel nothing?' is affective; it is a moral question and implies a value judgement. In the above quotation, Supple is using a moral question, 'How could human beings dump a truck-load of babies into a burning pit and appear to feel nothing?', to state the importance of teaching the Holocaust in *history* lessons. The Holocaust is a human story that forces us to confront the limits of human behaviour. However, there is debate regarding whether the moral lessons should come from historical lessons or vice versa. Richard J. Evans suggests that what is required to understand phenomena such as Nazism and the Holocaust is 'detachment'. He writes 'the historian has to develop a detached mode of cognition, a faculty of self-criticism and an ability to understand another person's point of view' (Evans 1997: 252). In the preface to a later book, *The Coming of the Third Reich*, Evans goes further, explaining that he views many of the histories previously written on the Third Reich to be contaminated by the rage or horror of their authors:

> It seems to me inappropriate for a work of history to indulge in the luxury of moral judgement. For one thing, it is unhistorical; for another, it is arrogant and presumptuous. I cannot know how I would have behaved if I had lived under the Third Reich, if only because, if I had lived then, I would have been a different person from the one I am now.
> (Evans 2003: xxi)

However, more than half of the history teachers I interviewed as part of this work emphasized the importance of moral lessons in preference to teaching the history of the Holocaust. It might be difficult to isolate the history of the Holocaust from emotional and moral considerations, but according to Nicolas Kinloch this is exactly what history teachers should do:

> We should teach the Shoah[3] in schools. But I do not think that history teachers will really do so effectively until we have removed it from its quasi-mystical associations and clarified our own objectives. I think we have to start and end with what happened and why, with the Shoah as history.
> (Kinloch 1998: 46)

When Kinloch asked a group of teachers why young people should be taught about the Holocaust, they responded that the Holocaust is possibly *the* critical event of the twentieth century; it changed the way we view Germans, Jews and human beings' capacity for destructiveness. All of the teachers Kinloch spoke to believed there were important moral, social and spiritual lessons to be drawn from the Holocaust and thought that studying the Holocaust improved students' ability to recognize and respond appropriately to similar events. However, Kinloch notes the problem with these objectives is that they are 'a dangerously non-historical set of assumptions' (Kinloch 1998: 44–5).

The Holocaust is an emotive subject. It took place within living memory in a modern, industrialized country in Europe. It is perhaps unsurprising, therefore, that history teachers' treatment of the Holocaust includes social and moral issues. However, in an unpublished review of Glanz's *Holocaust Handbook for Teachers: Materials and Strategies for Grades 5–12* (2001), Kinloch takes issue with the author's view that the Holocaust should be studied in order 'to encourage the growth of competent, caring, loving and lovable people'. Kinloch suggests that teachers of history might want to teach their students to do more than care. They might want their students to evaluate source material rigorously, to develop and demonstrate a clear understanding of concepts such as causation and to be able to detect bias and propaganda. Kinloch's difficulty with history teachers dealing with moral questions is that he does not see that it is their role to create a new society. But there are others who disagree. Steve Illingworth has criticized Kinloch's position 'as unduly pessimistic and lacking in ambition'. He has written, 'it is surely not too idealistic to hope that a study of the Holocaust would lead to pupils reflecting on their own behaviour and attitudes' (Illingworth 2000). Similarly, Terence McLaughlin has questioned whether the historical and moral and social lessons of the Holocaust can be separated (McLaughlin 1999) and Michael Meagher has written:

> Nicolas Kinloch draws too stark a division between the twin journeys of moral development and intellectual enquiry. Confronted with the real horror of the facts of genocide, the traces of the real suffering in physical, written, visual and oral evidence, is it not inevitable and natural that pupils will be disturbed into reflection of a deep and personal kind? (Meagher 1999)

While Kinloch is critical of history teachers who teach the Holocaust from a social and moral perspective, Stephen Smith, Director of the Beth Shalom Centre in Nottinghamshire, implies criticism of history teachers who fail to address the social and moral perspective: 'many teachers with whom we come into contact convey the Holocaust sensitively to their students. However, there are also many who ... are purely historical in their approach' (Quoted in Moloney 2003).

Paul Salmons, Co-ordinator of Holocaust Education at the Imperial War Museum in London, suggests that the objectives of teaching the Holocaust:

can vary depending on the class and the teacher's interest. Pupils need the narrative, a firm understanding of the historical events; causes and consequences; the teacher needs to generate interest and engender a genuine empathy. All of the victims need to be understood and explored without introducing any elements or reference to comparative suffering. The choices made by individuals at the time need to be explored, stereotypes should be broken down. There needs to be historical analysis, we must get beyond 'quasi-mystical associations', the Holocaust was a human event with human causes; there should be an exploration of the perpetrators, victims and bystanders, without 20th-century armchair judgement or condemnation.
(Interview, 12 September 2002)

Like Evans, Salmons comments on the need for detachment. The first line of this quotation is also interesting; Salmons recognizes the diversity of practice in the history classroom. The kind of study that is suggested here would take time, and there exists the danger that if insufficient time is spent teaching the Holocaust that stereotypes will actually be reinforced.

I have observed a Post-graduate Certificate in Education (PGCE) History student explaining to a 'low-ability' group of Year 9 students that there was once a very bad man called Hitler, who lived in a country called Germany and who did not like Jews. During the Second World War he tried to kill all the Jews who lived in Germany and in the other countries he invaded. The activity that followed was from a Heinemann publication, *The Era of the Second World War*. Students had to fill in the missing words: 'the Holocaust was the killing of ____ million Jews by the Nazis. Some were ____ . Others were herded into ____ and gassed' (Reynoldson 1993: 45). During a lesson later in the term with the same group, students reacted negatively to the suffering and death of German refugees; they believed that the Germans 'deserved what they got' because of what they did to the Jews. As the late Robert Phillips noted, quoting from Sean Lang (1999: 24), 'history "promotes notions of tolerance" [but] it is equally true that it can also encourage racism and prejudice' (Phillips 2002: 148).

There is equally concern regarding the dominance of 20th-century history in schools. In an article which appeared in the *Times Higher Education Supplement* (*THES*) Ian Kershaw was quoted on the reaction of Cambridge undergraduates to the dominance of Nazism in the school curriculum, 'they've had enough of it by the time they get here'. He went on, 'you have good students who have a detailed knowledge of Nazism but are worryingly uninformed about their own country's history or the aspects of German and

European history that would put that knowledge of the period between 1933 and 1945 into context' (quoted in Richards 2003).

While the objectives suggested above by Salmons are historical, others, like Short, suggest a range of further motivations for teaching the Holocaust. Short argues that the teaching of the Holocaust is helpful in explaining the situation in the Middle East, learning about the psychology of prejudice, helping to understand human behaviour, combating anti-Semitism, racism and prejudice and preventing future genocides (Short 1998: 10–15). Similarly, a number of motivations for teaching the Holocaust are suggested in a teaching guide produced by the United States Memorial Museum, *Teaching about the Holocaust: A Resource Book for Educators* (2001). These motivations are summarized here:

- the Holocaust was a watershed in the history of both the 20th century and humanity; a study of the Holocaust helps to promote notions of tolerance and diversity; the Holocaust provides an example of what can happen if no one speaks out; a history of the Holocaust demonstrates how a modern industrialized nation can utilize technology and bureaucracy to implement destructive policies; a study of the Holocaust prompts students to think about the use and abuse of power and the roles and responsibilities of individuals, organizations and nations in the face of civil-rights violations; students can learn to identify the danger signals and how to protect the democracies they live in.

While a number of the motivations suggested here and by Short are non-historical, they seem appropriate for teaching about broader social lessons. The only motivation suggested here and by Short which is immediately problematic is that of genocide prevention. As Kinloch has written:

> We could tell our students, 'Don't negatively discriminate against minority groups in society lest, at some unspecified date in the future, you stand idly by or actively participate in the deliberate extermination of one or other of these minorities. We can't, of course, tell you what other opinions might be available to you in these circumstances. But we're sure that now you've seen these photographs of Belsen, you'll do the decent thing.'
> (Kinloch 1998: 45)

In Germany, all students study the Nazi period and the Holocaust, but this has not prevented a rise in racism and neo-Nazism among the youth of Germany. In fact, the implication in one article published in *History Today* in 2001, is that it may have prompted it. According to Thomas Lutz, head of Memorial Museums for the Topography of Terror in Berlin:

Twenty years ago right-wing extremists would attack the evidence historians had about Nazi crimes. Now they have started conceding they did
happen and then saying what the Nazis did was right. Not only do they
say this, they write it in the visitors' books. It's only a small minority but it
is a new situation.
(Quoted in Fawcett 2001: 16)

Lutz attributes this to the development of a 'negative memory'. His view
was supported by a German history teacher: 'the fact that we can't look
back on the last century with any pride is certainly difficult for some young
people. Kids want to be proud of something and need to identify with something'. Several history teachers noted in this article that their students were
asking more 'revisionist' questions. The worry for Herr Lutz is the effect that
the upsurge in neo-Nazism among young people in Germany 'is going to
have now and in the future' (Fawcett 2001: 16–17). This article raises
the question of whether teaching the Holocaust is an antidote to racism
and prejudice.

In 1997, a survey was conducted of 7,927 students, at 120 schools, in
60 towns in Sweden. Incredibly, it reported that 'a third of Swedish 12 to
18 year olds do not believe the Nazis' extermination of the Jews ever
occurred' (reported in the *TES*, 4 July 1997). John Fox has written in *The
Holocaust Encyclopaedia* (Fox 2001) that throughout Europe the Holocaust
is studied at school and university level with varying degrees of attention being given to the subject from country to country. He concludes his
entry on 'Holocaust Education in Europe' writing that this 'reflects posi-
tively on the intention in Europe to resist any resurgence of National Socialism and other extremist movements based on racism' (Fox 2001: 305). But
despite the commitment to Holocaust education of governments across
Europe, the views of the German and Swedish students above would seem
to indicate that Holocaust education is not an inoculation against racist and
anti-Semitic propaganda. This brings us back to Kinloch (1998, 2001b)
and the question of whether teaching about the Holocaust can prevent
future genocides.

In terms of the moral and ethical questions that will arise in the history
classroom on the subject of the Holocaust, Salmons notes that it is important to find a way of dealing with these questions and not leaving students
'hanging'. Some could be very deeply affected – 'we subject our students to
events that may cause powerful emotional responses and so we have a duty
to help them express these feelings and to work through them' (Salmons,
correspondence, 29 September 2005). This is the same point that Meagher
has made in *Teaching History* (1999): if we expose students to a study of

human suffering, we have a responsibility to guide them through it. But is this the role of school history?

Before outlining the content of each of the book's five chapters, it is important to make clear what this book is not about. Research involving the Holocaust is closely scrutinized and is fraught with accusations of anti-Semitism; it is an area that has become highly politicized. This book considers

- how the topic of the Holocaust is currently being taught in school history in England; terminology and uniqueness; the way in which Holocaust education was moving prior to the introduction to the National Curriculum in England in 1991; how the Holocaust came to be included in the National Curriculum for history; and how the topic of the Holocaust has subsequently gained prominence.

This book is not about trying to diminish the importance of the Holocaust. It does not question that the Holocaust should be taught in schools, but encourages discussion of, and makes a contribution to the debate on how the Holocaust should be taught.

In an article about teaching the Holocaust, Moloney (2003) – who used a quotation from a letter I had written to *Teaching History*, 'the key to teaching the Holocaust well is not having more time but being clear in our own minds of our objectives' (Russell 2001) – wrote:

> The main problem seems to be that teachers are unclear about why they are teaching the Holocaust. Is the rationale behind it primarily historical, moral or social? Is the Holocaust to be taught as a historical event, with a view to developing students' critical historical skills, or as a tool to combat continuing prejudice and discrimination?
> (Moloney 2003)

Chapter 1 is based on interviews with ten teachers of history. It presents and considers current practice in the history classroom, which supports Moloney's assertion. The views of educationalists and academics are debated along with teachers' views in this chapter, which reveals a lack of clarity regarding the central aim of teaching the Holocaust in history. Throughout my research I have been struck by the lack of consensus regarding the purpose of, and approaches to, teaching the Holocaust in school history. The majority view is distinctly non-historical; there is a tendency to teach the Holocaust from a social and moral perspective and not as history. The proceeding chapters will attempt to explain and debate this phenomenon.

In September 2001 a special edition of *Teaching History*, which focused solely on teaching the Holocaust in history, was published. The editorial began, 'it is unusual – it may even be unprecedented – for an edition of *Teaching History* to devote itself to the teaching of one historical topic' (Counsell and Kinloch, 2001). This edition contained a deliberate range of contrasting perspectives and views on the topic of the Holocaust, making manifest the central question, 'Is the rationale behind the inclusion of the Holocaust in the National Curriculum for History historical, social or moral?' It is perhaps unsurprising that history teachers' approaches to the Holocaust are diverse, since there is a lack of consensus regarding the basic assumptions that underpin this teaching, such as, for example, what the term 'Holocaust' means. Chapter 2 considers definitions of the term 'Holocaust'; the question of whether the Holocaust is unique; and the implications of this debate for classroom practice. The chapter reflects on the impossibility of teaching the unique and learning something from this; 'the unique event is a freak and a frustration; if it is really unique – can never recur in meaning or implication – it lacks every measurable dimension and cannot be assessed' (Elton 1967: 11).

Chapter 3 traces the history of the Holocaust as a topic for study in the history classroom. It discusses the teaching of the Holocaust prior to the introduction of the National Curriculum and reflects on the work of the Inner London Education Authority (ILEA) in promoting Holocaust education. Materials produced by the ILEA, which were designed to encourage and support the teaching of the Holocaust, are reviewed and discussed in this chapter. The work being done by the ILEA in the 1980s remains relevant. In one lecture organized and videoed by the ILEA (ILEA 1985) and given by Clive Lawton (then Education Director of the Board of Deputies of British Jews), the issues of why it is important to teach about the Holocaust, what the term 'Holocaust' encompasses, possible pitfalls involved in teaching the Holocaust and ways that some of these might be avoided were raised and discussed. Before 1991, if teachers were going to teach about the Holocaust, they had to be convinced of the importance of this topic, since it was they who made the decisions about what they taught. The introduction of the National Curriculum meant that history teachers *had* to teach the Holocaust. The question of why history teachers *should* teach the Holocaust, a question that Clive Lawton had identified as being of primary importance in his 1985 lecture, appears to have been sidelined.

Chapter 4 takes as its focus the topic of the Holocaust in the National Curriculum for History. The Interim Report of the History Working Group, which was set up in 1989 to advise the Secretary of State for Education on the form the history curriculum should take, did not recommend the Holocaust – or the Second World War – as topics for study. This decision was reversed and the Holocaust was included, as an aspect of the Second World

War, in the Group's final report. But it is a curiosity that a topic that did not specifically feature in the 1989 interim report should subsequently emerge as a non-negotiable topic for study in its own right. Drawing on a series of interviews with members of the History Working Group and analysis of their working documentation, Chapter 4 examines and explains the Group's apparent 'U-turn'. This chapter demonstrates that a clear rationale regarding what was important about teaching the Holocaust in school history was lacking among those who developed the National Curriculum for history. It would seem from the evidence presented in this chapter that social and moral reasoning, more than historical criteria, resulted in the inclusion of the Holocaust in the History Working Group's final report.

Chapter 5 considers the topic of the Holocaust and its increasing prominence in school history since 1991. Margaret Thatcher resigned as prime minister in November 1990; she was succeeded as leader of the Conservative Party and prime minister by John Major, who went on to win the 1992 General Election. In 1993, his government announced the Dearing Review. This was set up to review and slim down the original National Curriculum, which, it was accepted was overloaded and over-prescribed. The slimming down of the National Curriculum for history was complicated by the fact that the subject was no longer compulsory at Key Stage 4 as had been envisaged by the 1988 Education Reform Act (ERA) and devised by the History Working Group. The School Curriculum and Assessment Authority (SCAA) Advisory Group for History were presented with the challenge of both slimming down and expanding National Curriculum content which, as one member of the Group recalled, 'in itself was a major issue' (Interview, 28 May 2003). A further curriculum review took place following the election of the new Labour Government in May 1997. The topic of the Holocaust emerged from this review as a topic in its own right, rather than as an element of the Second World War. According to Haydn, under the draft proposals drawn up by the History Task Group, the Holocaust was the '*only* topic specified by name which will be a compulsory part of the History Curriculum' (Haydn 2000: 135, emphasis in the original). This chapter also reveals that the opportunity to theorize the topic of the Holocaust has been denied those who have taken part in reviews of the history curriculum.

It is important at this point to note some of the methodological issues relating to this work. Chapter 1 draws on interviews with secondary-school history teachers. In September 2003, I sent out 40 multiple-choice questionnaires to history teachers in 20 schools in Kent, where I had taught. The questionnaire was designed to gain some basic information about interviewees and their approach to teaching the Holocaust. It comprised three questions relating to teachers' age, gender, and the year in which they qualified to teach. A further three multiple-choice questions followed regarding what motivated them to become a history teacher, what their prime objective was when teaching the Holocaust and what resources they used when planning and teaching lessons on the topic of the Holocaust. Finally, I was interested in whether the Holocaust was taught in other departments in their school. Nine returns were received in response; this number rose to 15 after a follow-up letter was sent out at the beginning of November.

Teachers' responses provided the basis for semi-structured interviews lasting between 25 and 40 minutes. Interview schedules comprised ten core questions:

1   What, in your opinion, is the purpose of school history?
2   You note that your prime objective when teaching the Holocaust is ____ Would you say that this is your sole objective?
3   Nicolas Kinloch has written in *Teaching History* that when teaching the Holocaust, history teachers 'should start and end with what happened and why'. How do you respond to this view?
4   Do you think the Holocaust is unique? Should it be taught alongside events such as the genocide in Rwanda?
5   Do you find teaching the Holocaust any more difficult than any other topics in history?
6   How many lessons are generally devoted to teaching the Holocaust in history? What is the duration of each lesson?
7   You have indicated on the questionnaire that you have found ____ useful in planning and teaching lessons on the Holocaust. How have you used this resource?
8   Have organizations such as the Holocaust Educational Trust made themselves and the services they offer known to you? For example, are you aware that they can organize for Holocaust survivors to come into school and give talks to students?
9   I am grateful you chose to take part in this research. Can I ask why you chose to do so? Have you taken part in any other research?
10   Do you read *Teaching History*? Do you find it useful?

Contacting the teachers who responded to the questionnaire proved difficult. In all cases, it was necessary to make several telephone calls, sometimes over a two- or three-week period, to teachers' schools. When contact had been made with teachers, school trips, forthcoming Office for Standards in Education (Ofsted) inspections and workload meant that interviews were difficult to arrange. However, despite the size of the sample, the data gathered has aided reflection on the teaching of the Holocaust in secondary-school history in England and has resulted in an interesting and important chapter.

Of the ten teachers interviewed, seven were heads of department. There were six men and four women, ranging in experience from newly qualified to 31 years. In Kent, a system of selection continues to operate: students sit a countywide examination at the age of 11 which determines whether they can apply for a place at the local grammar school. Two of the schools in the sample were single-sex girls' grammar schools; one of the schools was independent; one was Roman Catholic and drew students from across the ability range; one school had recently become a technology college and catered for students across the ability range; one was 'comprehensive';[4] and two were secondary modern schools. Both of the secondary modern schools faced extremely challenging circumstances and an uncertain future.

The teachers were guaranteed personal and institutional anonymity; their names have been changed. I interviewed Hank and Stephanie at their respective girls' grammar schools; Harold at the independent school; Leonard at the Catholic school; Anne at the technology college; Marie and Mike at the 'comprehensive' school; Barbara and Walter at one of the secondary modern schools; and Tom at the other secondary modern school. All but one of these teachers taught the Holocaust to Year 9 (13- and 14-year-old students). Independent schools do not have to follow the National Curriculum and Harold taught the Holocaust to Year 10.

Chapter 2 explores the issues of terminology and uniqueness, but for the purposes of Chapter 1 and the interviews conducted with teachers, the term 'Holocaust' – unless otherwise stated – includes any teaching that provides background to the Holocaust such as the history of anti-Semitism as well as the legalization of prejudice and discrimination by the State from 1933 onwards. Thus, Hitler's rise to power and events such as Kristallnacht are encompassed by this term.

Chapter 3 includes an analysis of the origins of the HET. This analysis, and reference made in Chapter 4 to individuals involved with the Trust and their actions, relies on documents obtained from the Trust's archives. These documents include

- a submission by Greville (now Lord) Janner Queen's Council (QC) and Member of Parliament (MP), John Marshall MP, Robert Rhodes James MP and Jeff Rooker MP on the *Teaching of the Second World War and the Rise and Fall of Nazi Germany in the National Curriculum for History*; letters from the then Secretary of State for Education, John MacGregor; documents relating to the establishment of the Trust and its early work;

and copies of questions asked in the House of Commons by Janner and John Marshall about the teaching of the Second World War and the Nazi period in schools. When drawing upon such materials, the issue of reliability is not the only concern – there is also the issue of authenticity. The authenticity of the various documents contained within the HET files could be assured in a number of ways: the covering letter sent with the submission from the MPs was written on House of Commons notepaper. The submission was reported on in a number of newspaper articles. The reply from John MacGregor was signed by the Secretary of State and written on headed notepaper from Elizabeth House, then headquarters of the Department of Education and Science (DES). The files also contained original letters from various individuals who had been approached to be patron of the Trust, again signed and on particular notepaper. Copies of newspaper articles and copies of questions raised in the House of Commons, which were found in the archives, were checked and cross-referenced with original newspapers and with Hansard. Documents such as drafts or copies of letters sent out by the HET (a number of which appeared to have been generated by Janner) could have been more problematic. However, there were letters in the archives that had been received in reply, which validated them. One question the historian asks is whether there is anything to be gained or lost by planting frauds, forgeries or hoaxes. The answer in this instance is 'No'. The HET is open and proud of its campaign to ensure that the Holocaust was a compulsory part of the school curriculum. I was requested not to photocopy letters from or to make reference to individuals who had written declining the invitation to become patrons of the Trust. This was to avoid causing embarrassment to the individuals concerned or to the Trust. These documents were not relevant to my study in any case. Given that I was allowed access to these documents and requested not to use them, it seems unlikely that anything would have been removed from the archives prior to my investigation of them.

This study has drawn on oral evidence from individual members of bodies established to advise on and review the content and structure of the National Curriculum for history. Interviews have been triangulated against each other as well as with documentary evidence including working documentation, letters from the time, semi-autobiographical works completed by History Working Group members (Guyver 1990, Jones 1991, Prochaska 1990) and newspaper articles. In addition to being useful for the purposes of triangulating data, there are other advantages to using oral and documentary sources alongside each other. Seldon and Pappworth (1983) see personal interviews as necessary for filling in the gaps in documentary evidence. Chapter 4 is based on original research that draws on interviews with individuals who served on the History Working Group, as well as their working documentation. These interviews provided data that was otherwise unavailable and gave interviewees the opportunity to expand on the minutes and to give their working documentation greater depth.

As with all methods of research, there are difficulties with regard to the conduct of interviews. Tosh explains, 'in an interview each party is affected by the other. It is the historian who selects the informant and indicates the area of interest.' He goes on, 'the presence of an outsider affects the atmosphere in which the informant recalls the past and talks about it' (1991: 213). Interviews were semi-structured and as relaxed and conversation-like as possible. The four key questions put to members of the History Working Group were:

1   Did you think that the Second World War and the Holocaust should be included in the National Curriculum for history? Why?
2   Do you recall why it was decided not to include the Second World War and the Holocaust on the interim report?
3   Why did the History Working Group change its mind and include the Second World War and the Holocaust on the final report?
4   Robert Phillips has suggested in his book, *History Teaching, Nationhood and the State*, that this change of heart was due to political pressure and refers to a question in the House of Commons (see p. 100). Do you recall any political pressure to include this period?

Tosh also highlights the limitations of personal memory (1991: 213). It is important to bear in mind when conducting interviews not only the fallibility of memory but also that interviewees, like politicians in their memoirs, may offer a particular version of events portraying their actions in a certain light. While this is interesting in itself, it is important, in order to be accurate, to have some corroborative evidence: 'oral evidence like all verbal materials, requires critical evaluation deployed in conjunction with all the other available sources' (Tosh 1991: 215).

It is not unusual for researchers to experience difficulty in gaining access to elites (Finch 1986, Hunter 1993, Ostrander 1993, Raab 1987). Perhaps access to History Working Group members was easier because they completed their work some time ago and, in a sense, they were former elites. I did not meet any serious difficulties in terms of access; all those I was able to contact talked to me. Members of the SCAA Advisory Group for History and the History Task Group were less willing to be formally interviewed.

While not essential, I would have preferred to name all the interviewees quoted in this book. However, my priority was gaining access to individuals, and I was prepared to offer anonymity where requested, mindful of Fitz and Halpin's assertion, 'we still think it is unlikely that civil servants would agree to be involved in policy research unless, or until, anonymity is assured' (1994: 36). Transcripts or notes made during interviews or meetings were sent to all interviewees to check and amend before any part of the conversation was included in the work. This was designed to gain the interviewee's trust and cooperation. I hoped it would also mean that I would be able to attribute comments to named individuals. However, as will be shown, history has proved a contentious subject in the National Curriculum. I raised some sensitive issues and, perhaps for this reason, some interviewees wanted their comments to remain anonymous. For this reason I, like Ball (1990), have quoted some interviewees but not others.

Access to the History Working Group's working documentation was gained with an offer from a member of the Group to borrow personal copies of this material. I am aware of documentation held by members of the History Working Group, some of which I have seen but do not have copies of, which I have been unable to make use of. However, historians researching any period can face this problem since no historian is likely to ever be in receipt of all the evidence relevant to their study. Indeed, history is a study of the past based on the available evidence. The benefit of completing contemporary research in this instance is that I have been able to talk to those involved in making history because they are still alive.[5] This book draws on contemporary history because it is through researching and understanding the recent past that the present is understood more clearly and that possibilities for the future become apparent.

Politicians' memoirs and newspaper articles have also been made use of in this book. Like all historical sources, memoirs should be carefully analysed, since politicians write these for a purpose: to provide their own account of their life and career and to defend or explain and 'put on record' their actions in government. The authors of these accounts are likely to be writing their memoirs some time after the event, using diaries and notes from their period in office. As such, certain additions can be made with hindsight. A quotation from Thatcher's *The Downing Street Years* comes to mind. Concluding her writing on the National Curriculum, Thatcher writes, 'by the time I left office I was convinced that there would have to be a new drive to simplify the National Curriculum and testing' (Thatcher 1993: 597). This may be true, but when Thatcher wrote this sentence in the first volume of her memoirs, published in October 1993, she may well have been aware of the announcement of the Dearing Review made in April 1993. Nonetheless, the memoirs of Thatcher and of Baker provide an interesting insight into the construction of the National Curriculum for History.

Newspaper reports not only provide a chronicle of events, but also attempt to shape them. Reports may contain the opinion of the journalist or take the political view of the editor or owner of the newspaper. It is important to bear in mind that all newspapers present contemporary events from a particular ideological viewpoint. This is particularly apparent in Chapter 5, where reports from *The Sun* and *The Daily Mail* newspapers are discussed.

The conclusion to this book draws together and reflects on the central themes and issues presented over the five chapters. The debate about what history teachers' objectives should be (historical, moral or social) is not resolved. What the book reveals is that there is a lack of clarity regarding the objectives of teaching the Holocaust in school history; the topic of the Holocaust is not being taught (and possibly cannot be taught) by history teachers solely as history, but often as something more like PSHE or citizenship. This tendency towards the social and moral is apparent not only in the history classroom, but is also mirrored at the curriculum decision-making level. In this sense, this book has something to say generally about how curriculum policy is formed and specifically asks the question, 'What is the rationale for teaching the Holocaust in school history?'

Chapter 1

History teachers on teaching the Holocaust

Teaching about the Holocaust goes beyond the usual considerations of lesson planning and resourcing. It is a topic that requires sensitive handling: how much detail should be gone into? How might students react? Is it appropriate to show images of dead bodies? As a history teacher, I found teaching about the Holocaust a challenge. Did my colleagues share my experience?

Do teachers have a clear rationale for teaching the Holocaust in history?

The views of the history teachers interviewed represented the spectrum of approaches to teaching the Holocaust. Teachers' approaches to the topic can be illustrated visually:

Historical   **Social and Moral**   **Emotional**

Harold Anne Leonard Stephanie Mike Hank Barbara Walter Tom   Marie

There was no consensus among the teachers interviewed about whether an historical or a social and moral approach should be taken. Rather, there was a range of opinion regarding the purpose of teaching the Holocaust in history, which tended towards a social and moral perspective. Given the nature of the topic, this would be understandable if school history was the only input students had on the Holocaust. However, the Holocaust was taught in citizenship, as well as history, in the school in which Mike and Marie taught. Barbara's school had a whole-school event on 27 January each year which had a social and moral focus, and in all of the other schools the Holocaust was taught in religious education (RE).

In 2003, Susan Hector completed a project entitled *The Holocaust in Secondary Classrooms: a comparison between the attitudes and choices of history teachers and religious education teachers*. She concluded that there was no significant

difference between the approaches of history and religious-education teachers to the topic of the Holocaust. This is to say that history teachers were
teaching the Holocaust from a social and moral perspective. Hector commented in her manuscript on the lack of guidance for teachers teaching
about the Holocaust: 'Teaching the Holocaust sensitively and effectively is
so important, and the pitfalls which can result in inappropriate teaching so
numerous, that it is surprising to me that there is so much leeway granted to
teachers' (Hector 2003).

In 2000 the Qualifications and Curriculum Authority (QCA) did publish
guidance for history teachers in the form of a complete set of schemes of work
for Key Stage 3. *Unit 19: How and why did the Holocaust happen?* (QCA 2000) is a
scheme of work that is designed to precede work on the two world wars and
the Cold War. However, this guidance is non-statutory and, it would seem,
it has had little impact on how history teachers approach the topic of the
Holocaust. Asked whether they had used this scheme of work, responses
from the teachers interviewed included

> It is quite recent isn't it, so it must have come my way. I couldn't com-
> ment on it because we haven't as a result made any changes to how we
> deliver it [the Holocaust] because of the cross-curricular links in Year 9
> ... So I couldn't say it's something that has influenced the way we work.
> (Stephanie)

> 'I haven't seen it' (Hank).

> I have scanned through it ... I did think about using it, but to be honest,
> once I had taught the Holocaust once and I saw what the pupils
> responded to, it was easier to look at what was going to get a good recep-
> tion from our students if you like, to look at what was going to benefit
> them. And I don't necessarily think the topics on the QCA scheme did
> that for our particular students.
> (Barbara)

None of the teachers interviewed used the QCA scheme of work. Asked
whether they took guidance from other sources such as the HET, teachers
gave a more mixed response. Barbara felt more confident in her teaching,
knowing that support and advice was available, while Harold was dubious:

> I tend to be a bit suspicious. I tend to throw the stuff away. We have
> found the Imperial War Museum exhibition is incredibly thought
> provoking, incredibly moving. Yet it is so well done because it isn't

propagandist in any way. There is a real attempt to provide a very thoughtful background explanation and you feel you're not being preached at. The message is clear without it being pushed in a way, because the whole thing is so powerful.

(Harold)

But the most interesting response came from Leonard:

They [the HET] have sent us some really good flyers, and the films are there, and the resources are there. I don't need the material. With something like the Holocaust you don't need vast amounts of material because the material will swamp what you are trying to get over, you will in fact stop teaching about it and all you'll end up with is a shock horror story. It [the Holocaust] has to have an intellectual dimension. It has to have a rationale.

(Leonard)

Leonard's comments call to mind a point made in the Introduction regarding the issue of whether the volume of resources available (many of which are cross-curricular and do not therefore provide a clear historical focus for the history teacher) actually help to focus lessons on the Holocaust. Hector expressed surprise at the leeway granted to teachers in this area. But what Leonard highlights is the need for teachers to have a rationale rather than more resources or greater guidance. But a rationale for teaching the Holocaust in school history is something which, as Chapters 4 and 5 illustrate, has been lacking since the introduction of the National Curriculum.

None of the teachers interviewed actually admitted feeling confused or unclear about their rationale. They all appeared confident about their own approach. I found this surprising. Prompted to consider my teaching by the reactions of my students, I had struggled with the topic because I found it difficult to separate and identify my main focus among a myriad of rationales.

However, there was evidence, among two teachers in particular (Marie and Stephanie), of divergence between what they claimed were their main objectives and what they did in practice. In response to the question relating to what teachers' prime motivation was, teachers could indicate one of the following rationales on their questionnaire or note another of their own:

- to help students understand and contextualize the Second World War;
- to give students the skills to detect discrimination, prejudice and racism;
- so that students are aware of this key event in 20th-century history;

- to remember the victims;
- to teach students about humanity and the capacity for evil within all human beings;
- so that students can understand why war criminals, despite their age, should be prosecuted;
- so that students can recognize and respond appropriately to similar events;
- to help students understand the current situation in the Middle East;
- to prompt students to consider and protect the democracies they live in.

Both Marie and Stephanie indicated more than one prime objective on their questionnaire return. This is unsurprising and interesting in itself. Indeed, one teacher from London, who completed a questionnaire as a pilot, had written in response to Question 5 'all of these – can't separate "prime" '. Based on my own experience and reading, I had expected teachers to find difficulty in defining a single prime objective and to indicate during inter-views that the Holocaust encompassed all of the objectives listed on the questionnaire and possibly more.

Marie identified three objectives on her questionnaire: to give stu-dents the skills to detect discrimination, prejudice and racism; to remember the victims; and to consider and protect the democracies students live in. I asked Marie whether she found it difficult to plan lessons for the time available that achieved these three objectives:

Last year, in my last school, it was a little bit easier because I taught RE [religious education] to exactly the same Year 9 group so we did quite a lot in RE about democracy and communism. I think you can tie in together objectives like protecting democracies and detecting the skills to recognize [state-sponsored] prejudice and racism. I always teach the Holocaust from the victims' point of view. I literally launched straight in because I only had two lessons so we didn't go through the whole, why did it happen or the consequences. I just said 'this happened'.

So you didn't teach about Hitler's rise to power or his policies?

No.

Which of the objectives you highlighted do you think is the most important?

From a historical point of view, I'd say to remember the victims.

So was the Holocaust taught in RE as well as history in your school last year?

No. I did it in history but I tied in some of the themes.

The discrepancy between what Marie believed were the key objectives of teaching the Holocaust in history and what she was actually teaching in the classroom, is evident. While Marie believed it was important to teach the Holocaust in order for students to consider and protect the democracies that they live in, she failed within her history lessons to teach her students anything about Hitler's rise to power, his policies and why these might have appealed to the electorate in Weimar Germany. It is unlikely that Marie's students actually learned anything about their own democracy and how to protect it, given that she did not teach them about how Hitler came to power and established a totalitarian regime. Marie's prime historical objective was 'to remember the victims'. However, to meet this objective, Marie used an ahistorical activity. She stated that she taught the Holocaust from a moral rather than a historical perspective:

> I want to teach the Holocaust from a moral point of view, not a historical point of view. I play the part in *Schindler's List* where people are going into the gas chambers without any volume but with Enrique Iglesias's 'Hero' playing very, very loudly. I tell pupils just to listen to the words and not to sing along and it's actually quite powerful sort of stuff. I've found it works really well. It gets me every time, I have to turn away. I can't watch it.
> (Marie)

Although Marie claimed to be teaching from a moral perspective, the activity described here is emotional. This experience contains no historical, moral or social lessons for students. The objective is simply to gain an emotional reaction. However, when I asked Marie whether her students reacted to this activity in the same way that she does, she replied, 'No. No. Most of them are more interested in the song'. There are two differences between Marie and her 14-year-old students. One is emotional maturity, but the other, which is more important, is that Marie is aware of the history of the Holocaust, but her students are not. Therefore, while Marie watches the images from *Schindler's List* and listens to Iglesias's song, she reflects on the events of the Holocaust. Her students lack that historical awareness. They do not know what they are being asked to remember and reflect upon.

Even though Marie did not claim she was confused about what her objectives should be, in practice, her teaching in this area lacked clarity.

Like Marie, Stephanie (who is German) demonstrated a similar discrepancy between what she said were her key objectives in teaching the

Holocaust in school history and what she taught in the classroom. On this occasion, however, the objectives highlighted were largely moral, while her approach was primarily historical. Stephanie indicated on her questionnaire that her prime objectives when teaching the Holocaust were: to give students the skills to detect discrimination, prejudice and racism; so that students are aware of this key event in 20th-century history; to teach students about humanity and the capacity for evil within all human beings; so that students can recognize and respond appropriately to similar events; to prompt students to consider and protect the democracies they live in. Given that all but the second of these objectives is moral and social, I asked Stephanie how she would respond to Kinloch's view that history teachers should, when teaching the Holocaust, 'start and end with what happened and why' (1998):

> I would largely agree with that view. I think it can be very dangerous for individuals, or individual teachers, to try and impose their own moral views on pupils. I would try to encourage expression of their views. When we teach the Holocaust in Year 11 we teach it in great historical detail at a mature level. We look at the historiography. We look at the historiographical debate surrounding the 'why'. Why could it happen? Could it happen again? Why did it happen in Germany and not in England? Could it ever have happened in England? Issues like that arise.
>
> I was very pleased when we went with Year 11 to the Holocaust Exhibition at the Imperial War Museum last year; I remember distinctly they were themselves raising questions such as 'Would I participate in this?' 'Would I be able to be a critic of the regime?' So I didn't even need to ask them this, but, of course, if it didn't come from them, I would foster discussion without necessarily giving my opinion and trying to be careful not to impose my own view.
>
> As a result of that, they quite often ask me my particular view, as a German. I always make it very clear it is my own subjective viewpoint and I'm giving anecdotal evidence at that point. I talk about my family's experience, well, my parents were babies at the time, but I talk about my grandparents' views. But I make it very clear that this is anecdotal because I think it's very hard actually to generalize people's experiences and therefore the sort of moral lessons which can be drawn from it.
> (Stephanie)

It is interesting that having indicated the objectives she did on her questionnaire Stephanie takes such a view. It would appear from her questionnaire return and interview that she believes there are social and moral lessons to be learned from the Holocaust but that these should be implicit and come from explicit historical inquiry. Her description of work completed with Year 9 students is evidence of this:

> In Year 9 the way we teach it is that we look at the experiences of the Second World War under the heading 'Human Suffering'. Because we know that in Year 9 in RE they will have already done a whole term on it basically, we don't feel we need to teach them in any great detail about the key events. And it would never be more than the key events because it is part of so many other things that happened.
>
> But basically what we do with them: the children are in groups and each group looks separately at an issue of human suffering. So maybe this would be things like the dropping of the atomic bomb, the fire bombing in Dresden, prisoner of war experiences and the Holocaust. And what they do is they make notes, they research it from lots of different books and the Internet. They each produce a piece of work on the topic they are studying. They've got a series of guideline questions to draw out the key points. They then make a presentation to the class about what they have found out.
>
> But I feel because they have already learned about the Holocaust I try to focus them in on the historical aspects, whatever group does it. I always try to give that particular topic to a higher ability group. Because I am extending them further I am quite sure I show them materials that I show to Year 11. I can't assume that they will take GCSE [General Certificate of Secondary Education] history; I even sometimes show them materials I would usually use with the sixth form. So they see lots of very shocking images. And I always try to pick out some mature girls to deal with that. But equally I try to steer them towards the 'why' and build them up to it. But each of the groups will have a moral dimension to their work and will in some way have to reflect on what that tells them about human nature.
>
> (Stephanie)

Barbara also identified more than one objective on her questionnaire return. She stated that her objectives were: to give students the skills to detect discrimination, prejudice and racism and to teach students about humanity and the capacity for evil within all human beings. This social and moral approach to teaching the Holocaust fitted with her opinion regarding the purpose of school history:

> The students that we work with are classed as 'sink' students, so we try and make history something they can be quite enthusiastic about.

We focus a lot on the social side of history rather than the factual – dates and things like that – because they can relate more to the social side. (Barbara)

There are those, like Kinloch, who might question such an approach. However, Barbara has a clear rationale and she and her department were clear about their motivations and objectives. Similarly, the rest of the teachers in the sample were clear about what they were doing and why. As can be seen from the discussion below, their objectives were largely moral and social, though interestingly, two teachers in particular (Harold and Anne) had a different view and taught the Holocaust for historical purposes in the first instance.

How diverse is current practice?

There is evidence of diversity within current practice. I was able to interview only two history teachers from the same department in two schools, though I had hoped more teachers from the same schools would participate. Barbara and Walter taught in the same school, as did Marie and Mike. Barbara and Walter worked closely together and taught to their scheme of work. However, there was evidence of some lack of consensus regarding approaches to and the purpose of teaching the Holocaust among history teachers within the same department. While Marie's approach was emotional, for example, Mike believed that:

What's important about the Holocaust is the banality of it. The thought that it could, in a lot of circumstances, happen almost anywhere and still does at times. And that it's not the Germans themselves but the set of circumstances perhaps that led to what happened. But also an empathy with the victims is obviously important and, if you like, a wider view of our responsibilities today to avoid discrimination is important. (Mike)

Mike's objectives are moral, but are rooted in history. Although Anne recently became Head of her department, she alluded to stark differences between her own approach to this topic and the approach of her former Head of Department:

I did a degree and my specialist subject was the Nazi Third Reich and I know there are a lot of people who take a very, very sort of, 'This is the

Holocaust, this is how we must teach it'. My previous Head of History was very much like that. I always wanted to kick back a little bit and say, 'Well I'd rather not teach it that way', and I kind of didn't teach it that way.

So how did your former Head of Department suggest you approach this subject?

It was much more emotive, a much more emotive approach. She used *Schindler's List* in chunks and looked at the emotive stuff, and I wanted to do it as a more source-based issue.
(Anne)

The question of whether the Holocaust should be taught from an historical, social or moral perspective is discussed in depth below. Before this, I want to highlight the issue of the amount of curriculum time spent teaching the Holocaust. Here, too, there was significant diversity.

How much time is devoted to teaching the Holocaust?

Brown and Davies (1998) identify the issue of too little time being devoted to the Holocaust. Salmons (2001) has also argued for a greater amount of curriculum time to be given to teaching the Holocaust. However, Tom had reservations about devoting more time to teaching the Holocaust:

How many lessons do you have to teach the Holocaust in Year 9?

I've got it down for four lessons. But I don't think I've ever done it in less than six. Lessons are 50 minutes long. I have – especially if I have shown *Schindler's List* or another film – run into eight lessons and we've done it in quite great depth.

So, within the six lessons you have in Year 9 do you look at Hitler's rise to power?

We do in the briefest of terms. We actually look at the rise of dictators. We look at Hitler, Mussolini, Stalin and sometimes Franco as well. So we look at the rise of dictators in general. Most of that does tend to concentrate on Hitler. But I am very well aware that we do tend to over-emphasize Germany and Hitler and, although it's a six-year period of history, in the scheme of things that's very small, and we spend an inordinate amount of time doing the First World War and the Second World War, when there are, maybe, events that have touched people just as much. For instance, we don't do the Space Race, the Cuban Missile Crisis. We hardly touch the Cold War. We don't really do the Russian Revolution either, and of course that had an incredible effect on the First World War. It could be argued the First World War was two years longer because the Russians pulled out. I just think we kind of overemphasize this bit.

Tom raises some interesting issues here. Like the two world wars and the Holocaust, the Cold War is a compulsory topic in the National Curriculum at Key Stage 3. But Tom notes that this is hardly touched upon. This is an issue many history teachers will recognize. Anecdotal evidence suggests that because the 20th-century world is taught about in chronological order, ending with the Cold War, time often runs out at the end of Year 9 and this history is left untaught. Despite the fact the Cold War features as a named topic in the History Curriculum there are students leaving school having been taught nothing about this.

To understand the Holocaust, students need to understand something about Hitler's rise to power and the history of anti-Semitism. Anne explained that:

> Although the Holocaust has to be taught in the unit at some point, I try and break it down. So when we talk about the invasion of Poland we do certain elements of genocide, so the idea is broached. And we also look at Stalin's genocide of the Poles for example, so that they've got some idea of context and some idea of development and how this is not just one man waking up one day and saying, 'Right, let's kill all the Jews on planet earth'.
> (Anne)

Anti-Semitism was a pan-European issue, connected with the eugenics movement whose ideas were popular in the USA and Britain at this time (Griffiths 1983, King 1999). Anne warns that if students do not have an opportunity to learn the political and social context in which the Holocaust is situated, they could very well be left with the impression that Hitler was alone in his anti-Semitic philosophy and that this was a solely German issue. Tom was concerned about oversimplification and about students having only a limited understanding of the wider picture. Barbara also identified the issue of students' negative attitudes towards refugees but – like Short (1998) – she saw the Holocaust as helpful in countering this prejudice, while Tom was of the view that if mishandled, this topic could in fact contribute to students' prejudice:

In view of resources it is also difficult . . . it's very difficult finding the balance between how much we give the students so that they understand how terrible this was, and giving them too much so they are absolutely shocked and horrified and really quite traumatized by the whole thing. I would like to try and strike a balance somewhere between the two, so that they don't get blasé about the whole thing, yet they are not totally traumatized by it and we develop anti-German feeling.
(Tom)

Barbara and her department spent 16 hours teaching about the Holocaust, having *already* taught the rise of Hitler and looked at his policies. For Walter, a newly qualified teacher, this did not appear to rest easily. He commented, part-way through the scheme of work on Nazi Germany, and a fortnight before Holocaust Memorial Day, 'I've done Hitler to death with my lot'. Walter felt strongly that there was an overconcentration on the Holocaust to the near exclusion of topics such as the Russian Revolution:

It really, really surprises me that no one spends any time on Stalin . . . the Holocaust is a lot more publicized than what happened in Stalin's Russia. But the Holocaust isn't the only genocide that happened. No one covers the British activities in Africa either. I actually skipped teaching the Russian Revolution altogether with Year 9 because I had three weeks to do it, but most of my degree was on Russia, I'm not going to get through it in two or three weeks.
(Walter)

Anne devoted between ten and twelve 50-minute lessons to the Holocaust, having already completed work on the rise of Hitler and Nazi Germany.

This level of concentration on Hitler, the Nazis and the Holocaust would, at first glance, seem to question the findings of those such as Brown and Davies (1998), Short (1995) and Supple (1992) who have highlighted the issue that, with some exceptions, there is too little curriculum time being devoted to the study of the Holocaust. Within the media the impression is similarly one of an overconcentration on Nazi Germany. As was noted in the Introduction, Ian Kershaw has been quoted in the *THES* on the response of Cambridge undergraduates to the dominance of Nazism on the school curriculum, 'they've had enough of it by the time they get here'. Twentieth-century history is the most popular choice of syllabus at GCSE. But in Year 9, which is the last opportunity for all students to learn something about the Nazi period before choosing which subjects to continue with to GCSE examination, the approach taken in the two schools discussed above, where a good deal of time is devoted to the study of the Holocaust, is not universal. Like Brown and Davies (1998), Short (1995) and Supple (1992) this study indicated that while some schools spent a good deal of time teaching the Holocaust, in others the time devoted to teaching this topic was not as great. Stephanie, as we have seen, teaches the Holocaust under the umbrella of 'Human Suffering' with students writing presentations on topics including the Holocaust. Hank has three or four double lessons (each lasting 1 hour and 10 minutes) in which to teach the Holocaust; Mike and Marie have '2 or 3 hours maximum really' (Mike).

Are students too young to be confronted by the topic of the Holocaust? The question of intellectual maturity

Leonard does not always teach the Holocaust at all: 'the important point to bear in mind is that if I haven't got enough time to deal with it adequately, then I don't'. The Holocaust is not an easy subject to teach, and Short has noted, 'it is debatable whether covering the Holocaust superficially is preferable to not covering it at all' (Short 1995: 187). This is very much Leonard's reasoning:

> I tend to introduce the notion of the Holocaust actually from past historical experiences that the kids have come into touch with. For example, outbreaks in the Middle Ages during the time of the Black Death, early medieval persecution, the exclusion of Jews from the guilds, this sort of thing, as background. It provides students with depth, in other words it gives them the idea that racism is historically inherent in European society.
>
> Also, we introduce elements of our own past records of racism, slavery for example, and present-day examples from popular press, popular issues that are arising. That's the angle I would tend to go in from, because to introduce the Holocaust as part of German history or, if you like, European history, having created the strand, I think you have to put it into the historical context in which it exists. That is as phenomena, an acute phenomena or extreme example of racism, but rationalized for the first time by a state, it's not ad hoc – spasmodic – like the persecution of the Jews in Russia or Poland for example. It's inherently a theology with its own logic.
>
> And that makes it extremely difficult because if you put it in the context of the war as well, I think it's confusing, it's too much for the students – especially Year 9. I tend to teach it as a separate study but cement it into

the Second World War and also the rise of a particular German ideology which grew out of an existing racism in Austria and Germany and Poland, it was inherent in middle Europe anyway.

The real problem with it – it's so horrific and it's so massive and it's so huge – is actually trying to make it appear not like a horror story, *Alien* or something like this, this is the problem. So if I haven't got time to deal with the background, because it is shocking and it is frightening, then I won't deal with it. I will just perhaps mention it en passant, it will be part of perhaps a series, a couple of lessons within the main history of the Second World War. A sort of awful but inevitable by-product of Nazism. But I won't deal with racism, the eugenic theories, persecution of groups, nor the way I suppose it stirred up racism in other European countries as well.

That's what's distressing, I suppose, to me or to the students, the fact that ordinary people – if you look at the European dimension to it – so many people seem to have cooperated and collaborated passively or actively with the Final Solution as it evolved. The impact of that could be so frightening and terrifying to some children that I wouldn't deal with it unless I had a lot of time to deal with it sympathetically and to steer away with it or close it down if I found they found it too distressing. So in other words you have to edit it, you have to be very careful. This is one area of history you really have to edit, I mean you can deal with sex and violence and murder and rape and all the rest of it because that's almost daily news. But the Holocaust isn't.

(Leonard)

Leonard highlights two key issues here: the complexity of the topic and the fact that history teachers have to teach about the Holocaust to 13- and 14-year-old students who do not necessarily possess the emotional or historical maturity to cope with such a study. Unlike Marie, Leonard teaches the Holocaust from an historical perspective – not an emotional one – and he is concerned when teaching the Holocaust to be aware of the reactions of his students to the topic:

If you want to get an emotional response, all you would need to do is select a few items of evidence, a few stills from Belsen, a few war diary reports from soldiers who were there and just let the evidence speak for itself. And then you could take a rhetorical emotional line. Emotion is always involved in history, I think, because if you don't have some value for it then your own emotion is involved. I would never teach just to shock and get them [the students] to cry. But if the emotion gave me a reaction that helped me to cement other ideas about causation or consequences for modern events, then I would use it. But I would never teach specifically to shock, it would not be an integral part. But anyway you can't avoid it in dealing with matters of conflict. It arises in every aspect of history that we teach. You could deal with the treatment of children in the factories and there is emotion there, there is an emotional dimension there, because if it wasn't for emotion then there would be no Factory Acts. So I wouldn't say so much *emotion* but *value*. Fellow feeling – empathy is the awful word to avoid because 21st-century children can't empathize with 1940s ghetto children from Poland, but they can at least see that they're fellow humans – they wouldn't be able to understand the point of view or perspective, but they could certainly understand it as children what it would have been like, I suppose.

But I think if you were to teach just for shock and horror you would have parents start complaining, you'd have nightmares. For example, I had a phone call from my own daughter, my granddaughter had come home from school crying her eyes out on Remembrance Day because she thought there was going to be another war; they had overdone Remembrance in her primary school. And being quite an imaginative little girl, she actually thought her daddy was going to be sent off to fight. Somebody somewhere made a mistake, and I think that's the sort of thing you have to be aware of very much.

I can remember German aircraft flying over although I was very small. Our folk history is different from the folk history of your generation. I think the subject is emotional and it's going to come out anyway, but if you deliberately go for the emotion then I don't think you are teaching history, because history is making sense of the past.
(Leonard)

What is interesting about Leonard is that he remembers the Second World War as a small boy. One might expect, because of his age and his memories, that he would be among the most committed to finding time to teach a detailed scheme of work on the wars and the Holocaust. But Leonard is aware of the complexity of this history and does not want to teach about this unless he has the time to do justice to it and is convinced that his students have the emotional and historical maturity to cope with such a study.

Like Leonard, Stephanie had concerns regarding the suitability of the Holocaust as a topic for historical study in Year 9. Stephanie's practice reflects Meagher's (1999) view that through the historical, students clamber into the moral. But there is a question of whether Year 9 students are intellectually mature enough to do this. Stephanie appears to link intellectual maturity with an historical study of the Holocaust. She comments in quotations above, 'when we teach the Holocaust in Year 11 we teach it in great historical detail at a mature level', and, 'I always try to give that particular topic [the Holocaust] to a higher ability group [in Year 9]'. Stephanie also makes reference to the fact that not all of her students will be studying history beyond Year 9.

During our interview, Hank reflected on his early experience of teaching this topic. Again, intellectual maturity is linked to teaching the Holocaust in his comments:

> I managed to get hold of some pictures of when Belsen was first liberated and in my first job, which was at a comprehensive, I had a bottom set and I passed the pictures around and some of the lads were laughing and I lost my rag with them. Looking back, perhaps I shouldn't have done. I was 22, the lads were young, they were embarrassed. I show the pictures here, but in my last school I would then only show them to top sets. But I feel that I have a duty to show pupils what went on.
> (Hank)

What Leonard's, Stephanie's and Hank's comments reveal is a fundamental question about teaching the Holocaust in school history. The original proposals for a National Curriculum for History covered students to age 16. However, in January 1991 Kenneth Clarke, who was Secretary of State for Education from November 1989 until April 1992, announced that students would be able to opt to take *either* history *or* geography at the end of Key Stage 3. This led to 'a rather hasty reorganization [which] moved the compulsory topic of the twentieth century into the final year of compulsory history' (Brown and Davies 1998: 78). This book is about the teaching of the Holocaust as a mandatory topic in school history, but perhaps the central issue is not about coherent and consistent teaching on the topic of the Holocaust in Key Stage 3, but why there is no opportunity for all students to study the Holocaust in sufficient detail at a mature level.

Although Leonard was the only teacher to voice the fact that he did not always teach the Holocaust, it would seem from research conducted by Short (1995) that Leonard is not alone in this attitude. Short has written:

> Fear that students could not cope intellectually or emotionally was responsible for one teacher approaching the subject superficially, another not mentioning Holocaust denial, a couple refusing to show *Schindler's List* and a fourth failing to draw parallels with contemporary racism if he taught in an 'all-white' part of the country.
> (Short 1995: 186)

Two of the teachers interviewed also said they knew of colleagues who did not teach the Holocaust:

> I know other schools where the Holocaust is hardly touched on. Although I think it is my duty to teach the Holocaust, I think it should be compulsory in PSHE or somewhere like that; although not all form tutors are historians or RS [religious studies] teachers. But I think it should be compulsory.[1] I think it would be good to teach about Rwanda so pupils realize it's not just about the Jews. It's happened in other places at other times.
> (Hank)

> *You just said you weren't sure how much time other schools spent on the Holocaust, so were you aware that the schools you completed your teaching practice in were spending less time on the Holocaust?*

> The schools that I can think of did the Second World War and the Nazis. I think it was very quick, 'did this, did that, kill the Jews', then they moved on. They probably covered the Holocaust in one lesson. One was a Catholic school, and one was a school like this, and I think they were nervous about pupils' reactions.
> (Walter)

There are possibly a number of teachers who do not teach about the Holocaust in Year 9 who would not be represented in my sample. I wrote to teachers asking them their views about teaching the Holocaust – a mandatory topic – in history. It is unlikely that those who do not teach about the Holocaust would therefore contact me to take part in the study.

Teaching the Holocaust and reflective practice

There is a further issue concerned with time: the time available for history teachers to reflect on the teaching and learning of the Holocaust. Hank admitted that while he subscribed to *Teaching History* and 'looked at' the Holocaust special edition, 'I've got into a habit with Year 9 because I've got material I know works I haven't really updated it. It's time really, and the priority is exam groups'. *Teaching History* is an arena for history teachers to discuss and theorize their practice and to keep abreast of debates and developments in school history. Below are some of the responses of teachers interviewed from the state sector to the questions, 'Do you read *Teaching History*? Do you find it useful?':

I read for historical pleasure. In other words I don't turn the history I read for pleasure into classroom use. Most of the time it's not on the curriculum anyway, but, obviously, there are times when you can draw on your past knowledge and you're unconscious of it, it creeps into your lessons sometimes. I do read historical journals, I watch historical films, I do read the magazines, but I would tend to say I read more books than anything else.
(Leonard)

I wouldn't say I read every article in it every month or every time it comes out. Yes, we always draw on it; sometimes we even use it with the students. We subscribe to it in the department.
(Stephanie)

I have them. They are in the cupboard, but I haven't read them.
(Anne)

I remember using it to complete assignments during my PGCE.
(Marie)

I probably haven't looked at it for years. What I have had is the *Modern History Review* and that's quite good. But we've not subscribed, so I don't read.
(Mike)

Every now and then I flick through it and try to get some new ideas. But I don't have as much time as I'd like to read it. In schools you don't have time. You're bogged down with paperwork, aren't you?
(Barbara)

Only for essays [at college last year]. But the tutors did sometimes photocopy things for us to read and put them in front of us, then I'd read it. Some of it was quite good.
(Walter)

I found it [the Holocaust special edition] very interesting. It's one of those things that I have on my list of 'I must try to include this'.
(Tom)

Barbara, Marie and Tom all lamented the fact that a lack of time meant they could not read as much or as widely as they would have liked, and Walter commented that 'I don't really get that much time to read'. Marie said, 'I don't keep up on it [developments in history education] at all. [I read] a quality newspaper maybe once a week'. It is worrying that teachers do not appear to have the time to consider and reflect upon their own practice and upon debates in history education.

The Holocaust as history or citizenship?

Evans wrote in *The Coming of the Third Reich* that according to the latest edition of the standard bibliography on Nazism, the number of works on the Nazi period stood at more than 37,000 in the year 2000 (Evans 2003: xvi). As Kinloch (1998) has noted, the Holocaust is an increasingly specialized area of historical research. However, the views of the majority of teachers in my sample reflected those of the teachers Kinloch had spoken to. Six out of the ten history teachers I interviewed talked about the moral lessons of the Holocaust being of *primary* importance. This discrepancy between what is going on in academic history and what is going on in school history calls to mind a point made by Felipe Fernandez-Armesto:

> We have forgotten how to defend successfully history's privileged place in the school curriculum. We have forgotten how to keep fully in touch with history teachers in pre-university education and how to feed their work with awareness of the refreshing and enlivening effects of new research. (Fernandez-Armesto 2002: 150)

While academic inquiry in this area becomes ever more specialized and detailed, my research indicates that Kinloch's description of history teachers' approach to teaching the Holocaust is accurate in the majority of cases. He writes:

> History teachers don't in my experience, approach the Shoah as a historical question. They deal with it ... as a moral, social or spiritual one. Implicit in much teaching of this topic is a metahistorical approach: an acceptance of the Santayana cliché about those who fail to understand the past being condemned to repeat it. This is the Shoah as a paradigm or analogy, and history in schools as a crude piece of social engineering. Sympathize with, empathize with the victims, says this approach; and students will find it impossible to become Nazis themselves. (Kinloch 1998: 45)

This 'metahistorical' approach to the Holocaust was reflected in the comments of 60 per cent of the sample. Marie's view was made clear above:

'I want to teach the Holocaust from a moral point of view, not a historical point of view.' As the following extracts demonstrate, she was far from alone in this point of view: Hank said, 'as the quote from Edmund Burke behind my desk reads, "the only thing necessary for evil to triumph is for good men to do nothing". I do make the Holocaust graphic.' He went on to say that:

> Although it's history, it's also moral . . . I would challenge Kinloch. It's a moral thing. I probably spend three or four lessons on the Holocaust. The first gives some background and is historical but the others are from a moral point of view . . . Every year I get a couple of girls who cry, and it's not just for effect. They might be Jewish or they are affected by what we've looked at. I do make a big thing of these lessons. I set the scene and I'm very graphic.
> (Hank)

For Hank, teaching the Holocaust is moral and emotional. According to Tom, who in his answer to my first question, 'What, in your opinion, is the purpose of school history?', quoted Santayana:

> I think if you can get that moral perspective across that may well prevent any future atrocities. And if we can get pupils to look at things from a moralistic viewpoint, that hopefully will teach them to be more holistic and more inclusive of all types of people of all faith, colour and creed.
> (Tom)

Mike's argument in response to Kinloch echoes the view of Haydn (see below):

> You can say that history is completely amoral if you want to, if you get up onto a higher intellectual plane. But I think one of the things we are trying to do when we are educating children is create viable, well-balanced human beings, and I think every subject should be trying to do that. Not just in citizenship or English or in RPE [religious and personal education] but everyone should be trying to place moral dilemmas in front of children, to make children think of the consequences of what happens and to try and create children that will make the world a better place.
> (Mike)

According to Barbara:

> I don't think you can look at what happened and why without looking at it from a moral perspective. I don't think you can address the issues of mass genocide and what happens in the world today without looking at

whether it should have happened or not. I don't see how you can teach the facts without looking at the moral issues. Especially with the Government's stress on citizenship, because it is an ideal cross-over subject. (Barbara)

And finally, Walter:

I've never taught the Holocaust before but teaching it, for me, is really going to be a kind of empathy area. So the pupils understand what it was like so that they don't go and do anything similar, or they don't go and join up with some stupid party; which a lot of people will do if they are ignorant – the promise of everything being alright if we just get rid of these people. I don't want them to go through that. So it's really just so it doesn't happen again, so they understand. It's like when they make black [racist] jokes, I want them to understand what it means. And then they can decide if they want to use those jokes knowing the background to them. I'm not going to force my ideas on them, but they have got to understand what they are saying, the background behind these things. (Walter)

What is the response among educationalists and academics to the approaches taken by these teachers?

Of all the approaches adopted by history teachers in the sample, I found Marie's approach the most startling and worrying. In Haydn's view, the Holocaust *is* about moral and ethical education. He suggests that if the Holocaust is taught from a purely historical point of view, as Kinloch suggests, then students could miss some of the different dimensions to it. However, Haydn would not hold with Marie's approach. In a sense, Haydn's position is not so far removed from that of Kinloch, since Haydn argues for the Holocaust to be taught using 'the same questions which we would ask of other historical events' (Haydn 2000: 137):

Instead of 'this is what happened; wasn't it terrible?' we need to ask the usual general range of questions which the discipline of history requires, while remembering that there are differences between the purposes of academic history, and the purposes of teaching history to young people. We need to get beyond approach A ['This is what happened; wasn't it terrible?'] and towards approach B [asking historical questions]. (Haydn 2000: 137)

Haydn makes clear his view that the Holocaust is not a story about good versus evil, it is more complex. He writes that Karpf (*The Guardian*, 3 April 1999) suggests the Holocaust has been hijacked by those who want their Holocaust stories to be about the triumph of the human spirit over evil and adversity, claiming the most cited entry from Anne Frank's diary is 'in spite of everything, I still believe that people are good at heart'. Haydn argues that students should not be presented with simple conclusions about the Holocaust that they do not have to think about, but should, rather, study a range of individual experiences enabling history teachers to present students with important questions about the human spirit and human nature (Haydn 2000: 143). Similarly, Salmons is of the view that:

> Learning more about this history can shake people's assumptions about the world, and about human nature. It would be far easier to explain away the Holocaust as the work of evil psychopaths, but research shows that this explanation will not do: these crimes were committed, on the whole, by ordinary men and women, not by demons and monsters.
> (Salmons, correspondence, 29 September 2005)

Leonard also has difficulty with oversimplistic emotive approaches to teaching the Holocaust: it is easy to get an emotional reaction from students, but how much understanding will they have?

Salmons (2001) argues that teaching the Holocaust should involve an emotional link with history, but should not be about encouraging tears. His position is, in fact, only subtly different from that of Kinloch. Both are in agreement that an historical approach should be taken, but Salmons feels that this cannot be divorced from consideration of moral issues, because the questions we ask as historians are often rooted in our own moral concerns. However, he is wary of turning the Holocaust into a story of good versus evil and of 'distorting the past in service of the "moral lessons" the teacher may wish to convey . . . we have to seek our answers in the documents of time and according to rigorous historical method and analysis, not make the history the servant of moral instruction or social engineering' (Correspondence, 29 September 2005). This is an issue to be borne in mind when reading in Chapter 3 the quotation from Supple, 'you must make it [the Holocaust] mean something. You can get the kids thinking about their own lives and behaviour, like bullying and racism' (*Jewish Chronicle*, 19 May 1989). There may be universal lessons for students which relate to the Holocaust, but those universal lessons are not specific to the Holocaust, they can be learned from other examples of history as well. There is an argument that linking the Holocaust to issues such as bullying trivializes this history. According to Salmons:

Rather than Holocaust education being the panacea for racism, prejudice and other social ills, a study of this history is likely to show the complexities of these issues and that there are no easy answers. The Holocaust will not inoculate young people against racism and it won't offer us simple solutions. The Holocaust should be studied not because it is redemptive, but because it is historically significant; it should be studied as history, not as a moral lesson; and we should recognize the very difficult questions about human beings that it may raise for young people and give space for them to reflect on these.

(Salmons, correspondence, 29 September 2005)

So, like Kinloch, Salmons would argue that the history and historical context of the Holocaust is fundamental, but Salmons would add that moral concerns are an important part of a study of this history because they are part of the history:

People at the time faced moral dilemmas, they had choices, and the decisions they made shaped events. This is a key part of the history and trying to understand why they made the decisions that they did should be part of our historical study. We should introduce moral questions not to play at 'what would we have done' but to try and understand why people in the past – perpetrators, victims, rescuers, collaborators and bystanders, made the choices that they did.

(Salmons, correspondence, 29 September 2005)

In this sense, Supple's question, 'How could human beings dump a truck-load of babies into a burning pit and appear to feel nothing?', which I argue in the Introduction is a moral question, becomes an historical question.

Teaching the Holocaust as history

While a moral and social approach was popular among the history teachers interviewed, this was not universally adopted. Two teachers in particular were vehement in their opposition to this approach. Both of these teachers were prompted to take part in the research because of their concern that otherwise my experience would reflect that of Kinloch (1998) and would present a picture of school history where lessons on the Holocaust were informed by the 'metahistorical' approach Kinloch alludes to. When asked during his interview why he had chosen to take part in this research, Harold responded that he 'felt it was quite important that I did say it should be taught in the context of history and history teaching, and in the context of Nazi Germany. And it shouldn't be taught in some sort of way where it's put on a pedestal for almost propagandist purposes'.

He wrote at the end of his questionnaire:

> I feel strongly that history should be taught as an academic enquiry and not in the first instance as a tool in pursuit of other goals. However, it must remain that its teaching is about 'collective memory' and many of the skills learned are transferable into other walks of life. To teach history for political reasons will surely lead to horrors just like the Holocaust, even if those purposes at first sight might seem benign.
> (Harold)

Both Harold and Anne felt strongly that the Holocaust should be taught from an historical point of view, allowing students to draw moral and social lessons for themselves. Indeed, in the preface to *The Coming of the Third Reich* Evans appears to advocate this approach to history. He writes:

> The story of how Germany, a stable and modern country, in less than a single lifetime led Europe into moral, physical and cultural ruin and despair is a story that has sobering lessons for us all; lessons again, which it is for the reader to take from this book, not for the writer to give.
> (Evans 2003: xxi)

Harold argues, 'I would start from the purist point of view – that history is an intellectual academic inquiry – but say that some practical consequences flowed from it.' Anne is very much of the same opinion as Harold on this issue – the history should come first:

> If you try to remove the morality issue then you are going to get a proper study of history. The morality can come in later when you have all the information in front of you and you've discussed the sources and you have a personal opinion. But to *cloud* the judgement of students, who should be fairly open to that, is very dangerous. We don't teach history in that way for any other topic. And we shouldn't be teaching it that way for the topic of the Holocaust.
> (Anne)

In this, Salmons is in agreement with Anne:

> If awareness of the importance of individual action and inaction causes students to reflect on their own role in society, then all well and good,

but while it is our responsibility to support them in this reflection, it is not our right to shape the history in order that they arrive at the same conclusions as ourselves. Otherwise, we cease to be teachers and become preachers.
(Salmons, correspondence, 29 September 2005)

What might impact upon approaches to teaching the Holocaust?

Anne was the *only* teacher to discuss the work of an academic in relation to her classroom practice:

> I keep in contact with Dr Fox . . . He taught me when I was at university, so I keep my finger on his articles and things because he did broaden my mind. So whenever his stuff comes out I try and get hold of that from the periodicals. His approach made me think because he asked us 'How was the Holocaust equally difficult or demanding on a "normal" German citizen as it was on a Jew?' A lot of the things he taught me I have carried into the classroom.
> (Anne)

Indeed, Fox's reservations regarding the term 'Holocaust', which are highlighted in the following chapter, are reflected in Anne's comments:

> I don't like the word 'Holocaust'. I haven't liked the word ever since I studied it at university. It is a study of genocide. And the Holocaust is part of that genocide . . . And I much prefer to talk about genocide. I do make a point, when we first start studying the topic, of explaining to kids why I will be saying genocide, and using 'Holocaust' as a term in certain cases as opposed to all the time.

So how would you define the term Holocaust?

I would take that as meaning the execution of the Jews.

And then genocide?

As a broader issue encompassing all groups. And I would always try to make it clear to the students that the Jewish issue is genocide as well. And I always try to link it to, for example, Somalia and more recent conflicts and try and show them how ethnic cleansing is not just about

picking one group of people throughout the whole of history, but about the development of conflict with different groups of people. When teaching Nazi Germany, I always try and get the issue of Aryan race through. I try and feed the two lines together. It's not about what's not acceptable, it's more about what is 'perfect' or should be protected.
(Anne)

Anne was also the only teacher who raised the issue of terminology and stressed the importance of this. Anne is clear and confident in her approach. What we see in her comments is an out-and-out rejection of an explicitly emotional presentation of the Holocaust in school history. Anne's confidence appears to come from the fact that she has studied Nazi Germany at degree level. Her confidence contrasts Barbara's experience:

You mentioned feeling uptight about teaching the Holocaust initially; I remember feeling more aware about teaching the Holocaust than other topics. Why do you think that is?

I think perhaps it's because of the enormity of it. When we teach about other topics, they don't seem so huge. It is also because the Holocaust still affects people's lives today. We are trying to get a Holocaust survivor from the Holocaust Educational Trust down to do a talk. And I don't know the religion of all my students, but there is a chance there are Jewish students in the class who could have relatives who were affected. And I'm always very aware of that. And also in our school we have got refugee issues. And of course some of the experiences that we talk about could be similar to experiences they have had in their home countries.
(Barbara)

Barbara's comparative lack of confidence was also reflected in response to another question:

How did you find out about the work of the Holocaust Educational Trust?

Through their newsletter at my last school. We receive their newsletters. We have asked for an outside educator and a survivor this year. They've been really helpful.

Do you feel you need that support, or do you think there are enough resources?

I think it's quite nice to have an expert to go to because sometimes the children do come up with questions, and it's nice to think, 'I don't know,

but I can find out for you'. When I did my first Holocaust Memorial Day, I showed some images and one of the heads of year said, 'They'll all be having nightmares now'. And I thought 'Have I done something wrong?' so it was nice to be told by the Holocaust Educational Trust, 'No. Students need to know this. Children need to know this'. So it's quite nice to have a bit of back-up and someone to advise you.
(Barbara)

What Marie, Anne and Barbara represent are three key points on the spectrum of approaches to teaching the Holocaust in history:

Historical	**Social and Moral**	**Emotional**

Anne	Barbara	Marie

Future research in this area may address the question of whether gender has an impact upon how history teachers approach the topic of the Holocaust. However, my study would seem to indicate that it is not gender, but rather what teachers consider the purpose of school history to be, and the opportunity to study debate and reflect on the issues, which actually shape teachers' approaches.

Anne would appear to be in agreement with Kinloch. She rejects a social and moral approach to the Holocaust which takes the Jewish experience as the focus:

I try and get them [the students] to understand this concept that just as much as the Jews are being singled out, just as much as other minorities are being singled out, it is also the rights of the good German citizen that are being removed as well ... I don't particularly wish to join a line and preach. That's not learning.
(Anne)

Asked whether she felt more emotional when she taught the Holocaust than when she taught any other history, Anne replied, 'No, but I do know a lot of teachers who are and I do know a lot of teachers who will put *Schindler's List* on and cry at the back of the room.' In a quotation above, Anne raised an important issue regarding whether history teachers who make explicit links between the Holocaust and issues such as prejudice, discrimination and racism also make links to moral and social issues when teaching topics such as the Reformation and the Industrial Revolution: 'We don't teach history in that way [from a moral point of view] for any other topic. And we shouldn't be teaching it that way for the topic of the Holocaust.' Marie responded to the question, 'Do you find that you tend to teach any other topics in history from a moral point of view?': 'I don't actually, no. Whenever I do the wars, I try and keep it down the middle. It's only the Holocaust that I find that with.'

Does it follow that history teachers are clearer about objectives for teaching other areas of the curriculum?

Like Marie, the views of Hank, Tom, Mike, Barbara and Walter similarly reflected a citizenship or PSHE focus. In response to a request for an interview, Ann Low-Beer commented that the Holocaust was an interesting but difficult issue because it 'has become overlaid with non-historical issues. Or it can be seen in layers, the past entangled with the present' (Correspondence, 14 June 2002). Do teachers approach other areas of the Key Stage 3 History Curriculum specifically as history?

Research conducted by Husbands *et al.* between 1999 and 2001 indicated that topics such as the Holocaust and slavery were being singled out by history teachers as being important in terms of values education and, as such, taught from a moral perspective. During their research, a lesson on the topic of the Holocaust was observed. The authors set their discussion of this lesson and a lesson on the Black peoples of the Americas apart from their main analysis and discussion of the history lessons they observed because, 'in each case the teacher specifically identified the goal of the lesson as something other than historical understanding'. For the teacher teaching about the Holocaust, this lesson was 'more a citizenship lesson than a history lesson' designed to 'get the pupils to understand what man can do to man and so what their role in the future is in terms of being vigilant'. This teacher wanted to encourage 'a personal response which involved some thinking' (Husbands *et al.* 2003: 81). This is reminiscent of the approaches adopted by Hank, Walter and Tom in particular.

The research that this chapter is based on provides an insight into the present state of Holocaust-teaching in history classrooms in English secondary schools. This chapter has highlighted the fact that there is a lack of clarity regarding the rationale underpinning the teaching of the Holocaust in school history. However, this lack of clarity is not experienced by history teachers on an individual basis, as was my own experience and expectation. Rather, there is a general lack of clarity among the profession: history teachers hold differing views as regards the purposes of, and their approach to, teaching the Holocaust. Practice is widely varied, but, in the absence of a specific rationale, there is a tendency for history teachers to teach the Holocaust from a social and moral perspective, and not as history. The following chapters explore this phenomenon and attempt to explain how it has developed.

Chapter 2

What was 'the Holocaust'?

It is unsurprising that history teachers' approaches to the topic of the Holocaust are diverse and lacking a specific rationale, since there is a lack of consensus regarding the basic assumptions that underpin this teaching. Such as, for example, what the term 'Holocaust' means. Before completing this research, I had understood the term 'Holocaust' as a generic term for National Socialist genocide. There are those who support such a view. For example, Alan S. Rosenbaum refers to 'the Nazi-engineered Holocaust against the Jews, Gypsies and millions of others' (Rosenbaum 1996: 1). Similarly, Robert Stradling, in the Council of Europe publication *Teaching Twentieth Century European History* states:

> The term 'Holocaust' is used to refer to the annihilation of more than 16 million people by the Third Reich during the period 1933–45. Nearly six million victims were Jews, which represented over two thirds of the total population of European Jewry, and a quarter of the victims were children. Other victims included Polish, Russian and Ukrainian civilians and prisoners of war, the Roma/Gypsy populations, socialists, homosexuals and people with mental and physical disabilities.
> (Stradling 2001)

However this interpretation of the Holocaust is not agreed. For many, the term 'Holocaust' refers explicitly to the Jewish experience. Bresheeth *et al.* offer a definition of the Holocaust describing this as the Nazi attempt to destroy European Jewry, which was part of a vast operation of genocide encompassing millions of Gypsies, people with mental and physical disabilities, homosexuals and political and religious prisoners (Bresheeth *et al.* 2000: 3). The Holocaust Exhibition at the Imperial War Museum in London adopts a similar definition of Holocaust:

> Under the cover of the Second World War, for the sake of their 'new order', the Nazis sought to destroy all the Jews of Europe. For the first time in history, industrial methods were used for the mass extermination

of a whole people. Six million were murdered, including 1,500,000 children. This event is called the Holocaust.

The Nazis enslaved and murdered millions of others as well, Gypsies, people with physical and mental disabilities, Poles, Soviet prisoners of war, trade unionists, political opponents, prisoners of conscience, homosexuals and others were killed in vast numbers.
(From the Holocaust Exhibition at the Imperial War Museum)

During an interview with Paul Salmons, Co-ordinator of Holocaust Education at the Museum, he explained this definition:

In the work we do at the museum, the term 'Holocaust' is carefully defined to mean basically the murder and persecution of the Jews in Nazi Europe. When we talk about the Holocaust that's what we are talking about, the murder of 6 million Jewish people. To expand a little, although that's the way we use the term 'Holocaust', the exhibition explores the persecution of all victim groups.

The problem I have with saying all those who suffered under Nazi rule suffered in the Holocaust, is that it basically lumps everyone in as being the same, and rather than making things clearer, it makes things more muddied. What about civilians in London who were killed by Nazi bombs? Is that the Holocaust? I would say not. They were innocent people; they were killed because they were English if you like, living in London. But it was not a racial attack. If you want to limit the definition of Holocaust to people who experienced the camps, well what about those who were held in prisoner-of-war camps? People were treated appallingly in prisoner-of-war camps. Is that the Holocaust? I would say not. Those few British prisoners of war who were killed in Auschwitz, are they victims of the Holocaust? Well, no, they are not victims of the Holocaust in the strict sense of that term.

As soon as you start opening it up too far, it becomes very difficult. These people suffered tremendously, and their suffering isn't any less because they are not part of the Holocaust. I think the problem comes when people try and maintain that the Holocaust is somehow worse than all other forms of suffering. If you don't do that, I don't think there is a problem in saying that the Holocaust was the murder and persecution of 6 million Jews. It is only when you get into comparative suffering, and then say that the Holocaust was worse than the suffering of Roma, or homosexuals, or political opponents [that that definition becomes a problem].

Salmons went on:

> The Holocaust was the murder of the Jews, but if you are going to try to
> understand that, you also have to understand Nazi hatred of other groups
> as well. The Holocaust didn't happen in isolation, it didn't happen out of
> nothing. One example would be euthanasia. How can you really under-
> stand the Holocaust if you don't look at T4?[1] So, immediately, you're into
> the persecution of other groups as well, and the suffering of those other
> groups obviously shouldn't be minimized, they should be understood in
> their own right. But it is right to understand the persecution of people
> with disabilities, or the Roma, or homosexuals for the reasons they were
> persecuted, and not try and pretend it was the same as the Jews. So I
> wouldn't try to rate one above another, but I would say that the Holo-
> caust was the murder of the Jewish people ...
>
> Our exhibition starts in 1918 at the end of the First World War, then
> later on in the exhibition you go back even further and look at 2,000
> years of anti-Semitism as well, and see this as a European-wide phenom-
> enon ... In terms of what the Holocaust was, it's not just the murder of
> people in death camps either, it's the reasons why these things happened
> as well, it's the consequences of them, the way that people reacted to Nazi
> persecution. You obviously have to explore resistance groups; you have to
> explore the way that Jewish people reacted in the ghettos and camps; you
> have to look at different forms of resistance; you have to look at the experi-
> ence of other victims. It's all of these things. So, in the exhibition, and
> when working with teachers and schools, we look at a much broader
> area than that narrow definition.

Salmons' response demonstrates the enormity of the Holocaust as a topic for
historical study. T4 refers to the euthanasia programme that was carried out
by the Nazis between December 1939 and August 1941. This programme
was not about 'mercy killing' or 'assisted suicide' but was instead bound up
with eugenic ideas about racial purity and national health. About 50,000 to
60,000 children and adults from medical institutions in Germany who had
physical or mental disabilities were secretly killed, either by lethal injection
or gassing. The headquarters of this programme were at Tiergartenstrasse 4
in Berlin, hence the code name T4 (Milton 1976: 131). The gassing tech-
nique used to murder mentally ill patients would later be used as the model
for the gassings at Auschwitz (Rees 2005: 69). None of the teachers interviewed mentioned T4, and yet, as Salmons states, how can you really understand the Holocaust without looking at the euthanasia programme? Such
a study as that which is suggested by Salmons would take a number of

lessons. And time, as was highlighted in the previous chapter, is an issue. But more than the issue of time, what is important is that history teachers be clear about their objectives and have an *historical focus*.

What does the term 'Holocaust' mean?

The word 'holocaust' comes from the Greek; 'holos' meaning 'whole' and 'caustos' meaning 'burnt', so 'holocaust' can be defined as 'wholly consumed by fire'. Speaking on BBC Radio 4's *Word of Mouth* programme, David Cesarani explained that 'holocaust' is a Greek translation of a Hebrew word used to describe sacrifices in the temple (*Word of Mouth*, 6 May 2005). Bresheeth *et al.* note that originally the term meant a sacrifice consumed by fire, or a burnt offering. Later it came to mean 'a sacrifice on a large scale' and, by the late 17th century, 'the complete destruction of a large number of persons – a great slaughter or massacre' (Bresheeth *et al.* 2000: 4). Discussing the origins of the word 'holocaust', Cesarani noted that the term Hebrew and Yiddish speakers have used for the Holocaust is *Churban* (pronounced hur-ban), which is taken from Hebrew and means destruction or desolation (*Word of Mouth*, 6 May 2005).

The term 'Shoah' (pronounced sho-wah), preferred by some, including Kinloch, and popular in Israel after the Second World War, is Hebrew for 'a great and terrible wind'. According to Kinloch:

> I always use the term Shoah and mean the Jewish experience, and the more general genocide to cover *all* the victims of Nazism, including the Shoah. This leaves me free to accept the term holocaust to mean *any* example of deliberate mass murder: I'm quite happy to see such references as Mike Davies' when he talks about Late Victorian Holocausts.
> (Correspondence, 25 June 2002)

In 1953, Yad Vashem was established to commemorate the 6 million Jews murdered by the Nazis and their collaborators. During the 1950s, this organization decided to translate 'Churban' and 'Shoah' into 'Holocaust' for Anglo-Saxon readers on the basis that this word, with its Greek European root, was easier to pronounce (*Word of Mouth*, 6 May 2005).

However, Ann Low-Beer, who was one of the members of the History Working Group established to develop the original National Curriculum for History, feels the most appropriate term to describe the Nazi persecution of the Jews is 'the Final Solution' (*Endlösung* in German) since this is how the Nazi exterminatory policy was referred to by people at the time (Interview,

29 July 2002). But Cesarani suggests that one of the reasons for the popularity of the term 'Holocaust' is that it distanced those who used it from the events of history, making it popular among German speakers (*Word of Mouth*, 6 May 2005).

Although Ian Kershaw has commented that even in the late 1970s when the US television series *Holocaust* was broadcast, 'the word [Holocaust] itself was not so common' (quoted in Richards 2003). The word has become increasingly popular. In the United Kingdom, National Holocaust Memorial Day is held on 27 January each year, and in the USA there is an annual Holocaust Remembrance Day. These dedicated days of remembrance and the Holocaust Exhibition in London and the United States Holocaust Memorial Museum in New York are evidence of the fact that the word 'Holocaust' has, as Steven Katz has noted, 'become so much part of the landscape' (Katz 1994: 1). And it is because the term has become so much part of the landscape, and because this is the term which is used in schools and appears in the National Curriculum for History, that I have used it in this book.[2]

However, there are objections to the use of the term 'Holocaust'. Not least the notion that the Jews who lost their lives as a result of Nazi exterminatory policy were part of some sort of sacrifice. There is some degree of contention over the issue of whether the term 'Holocaust' encompasses all of the victims of National Socialism, as well as over whether it is an appropriate description of the Jewish experience. Amos Oz writes:

> I do not use the word 'holocaust' when I refer to the murder of the Jews of Europe. The word falsifies the true nature of what happened. A holocaust is a natural event, an outbreak of forces beyond human control. The murder of European Jews by the German Nazis was no holocaust.
> (Oz 1988: 19)

Elie Wiesel has also wrestled with the term, which he in fact may have been the first to use to describe the Jewish experience (Paris 2002: 330):

> I have seen it myself on television in the country in which I live. A commentator describing the defeat of a sports team, somewhere, called it a 'holocaust'. I have read it in a very prestigious newspaper in California, a description of the murder of six people, and the author called it a holocaust.
> (Wiesel 1988: 13)

The issue of terminology is important. In an interview with Fox, author of *Teaching the Holocaust: the report of a survey in the United Kingdom* (Fox 1989), he explained that he has not used the term 'Holocaust' for some years. Instead he talks about 'the Nazi persecution and genocide of the Jews' (Interview, 21 January 2004). This is because he feels the emphasis on the Holocaust, and therefore the Jewish victims of Nazi racism and genocidal policy, 'hides' the suffering and fate of millions of other victims of National Socialism. This is an issue.

The term 'genocide' was defined by Raphael Lemkin in 1943 as the planned annihilation of a people. Lemkin described genocide as a progressive process, a 'co-ordinated plan of different actions aiming at the destruction of the essential foundations of the life of national groups, with the aim of annihilating the groups themselves' (quoted in Paris 2002: 334). This definition therefore encompassed all victims of Nazi extermination policy. In January 2005, it was reported that the Muslim Council of Britain would boycott the 60th anniversary commemoration of the Holocaust in London because, according to the Council's Secretary General Iqbal Sacranie, the event did not acknowledge 'genocide' in the occupied territories of Palestine. 'In effect', wrote John Mullan, in a piece in which he highlighted the issue of language and the debate surrounding the meaning of the word 'Holocaust', Iqbal Sacranie 'is proposing that we return Holocaust to the range of meaning that it had up until the 1940s' (Mullan 2005).

The issue of the suffering of which groups was encompassed by the term 'Holocaust' was a live one during the design of the Holocaust Memorial Museum in New York.[3] Paris has written about the debate regarding the content of this museum:

> The Armenian-American community wanted recognition of its history, but some members of council [set up to decide the content of the Holocaust Museum] worried that including the Armenian story might open the door to recognizing other tragedies, such as the ravages of Pol Pot in Cambodia, or the massacres of North American Indians. The question was, who is 'in' and who is 'out'? Where were the boundaries to be drawn? (Paris 2002: 334)

Cesarani sees 'a great value in reverting back' to the use of the word 'genocide' in place of 'holocaust' to deal with this very problem of whose holocaust it is (*Word of Mouth*, 6 May 2005).

But there is an academic argument for abandoning both the term 'holocaust' and the term 'genocide'. Fox has difficulty with the term 'genocide', because, inevitably, people talk about definitions. The killing of Armenians by Turks was described by the British Prime Minister Winston Churchill as a holocaust just after the First World War. For decades, the Armenian people have been campaigning to have the killings of hundreds of thousands of their ancestors in Ottoman Turkey in 1915 recognized as genocide. This has been met with a determined campaign by the Turkish Government to deny genocide. In BBC 2's *Correspondent* programme, broadcast on 26 January 2003, Fergal Keane highlighted the broken promises to the Armenian people from both President Clinton and President George W. Bush. Both presidents had said that they would recognize this genocide, but Turkey's threat to withdraw military bases forced the American Congress to abandon legislation which would have used the term 'genocide'.

According to Fox, if different mass murders are categorized under different headings, debates develop concerning a hierarchy of victims, 'the problem is that any action of mass murder that does not fit that definition therefore can't be described as genocide. But then, how do you rate the memory of the fate of those victims of innumerable cases of state-directed mass murder in the modern world? Are they not worthy of memory?' (Interview, 21 January 2004). The uniqueness debate outlined and discussed below is linked to this issue of definitions. Stannard writes about the support received by the Turkish Government from the Israeli Government in the campaign to deny the Armenian genocide, noting that this relationship is quid pro quo:

> The Turkish Government has repaid these generous efforts on its behalf by publicly stating not only that (as their Jewish friends obligingly have confirmed for them) there was never an Armenian genocide but that the Nazi assault on the Jews was indeed historically unique. This is the process ... that Roger W. Smith has called 'denying genocide by acknowledging the Holocaust'.
> (Stannard 1996: 196)

The use of the term 'genocide' has implications not only for the memory of the dead, but for how we treat the living. The refusal of the West to define events in Rwanda in 1994 as genocide meant that the international community were not required to act under the 1946 Genocide Convention (Melvern 2000). Similarly, in the USA in July 2004, the House of Representatives said that what was going on in Darfur was genocide and that it should be called as such by the Bush Administration. But the White House and the United Nations were again reluctant to do so, because this would oblige them to act. These examples demonstrate the importance of language and definitions.

Is the Holocaust unique?

> Since the Second World War ended, there have been dozens more geno-
> cides in countries such as Rwanda, Cambodia, Iraq and the former Yugo-
> slavia. So what more can be done to ensure that the Holocaust is never
> forgotten and its crimes never repeated?
> (Crace 2002: 4)

In the previous chapter, both Tom and Walter commented on the lack of
curriculum time to teach about the Russian Revolution. It is in asking why
the deaths of 14.5 million kulaks is not a feature of school history that a fundamental question is revealed, 'Is the Holocaust a unique event in history,
or is it an example of an appalling act of genocide?' While the uniqueness
debate is not new in academia, it remains relevant in the history classroom:
there is a view that if the Holocaust is perceived as unique, then its status in
the National Curriculum for History is unquestionable. However, Kinloch
notes that 'a major problem for those who believe that we can avoid future
genocides by studying the Shoah is the issue of historical uniqueness' (Kinloch 2001a: 11). If the actions of Hitler and the Nazis are unique and incomparable, then surely it is impossible to argue, as Ian Gregory does, that
teaching about the Holocaust 'reflects our determination that never again
should such an atrocity be perpetrated' (Gregory 2000b: 50). By definition,
such an event could never be repeated. On the other hand, if the Holocaust
is an example of genocide, then there is a question about why this genocide is
exclusively included as a compulsory part of the History National Curriculum and why we do not spend more time teaching about other genocides.
Further, if the Holocaust is a unique *Jewish* experience, there are implications in terms of the attention given in history lessons to examining the
Nazis' treatment of the Gypsies, homosexuals, people with mental and physical disabilities, political prisoners and religious groups.

Between 1939 and 1945, millions of people died at the hands of the Nazis.
Among the victims were 6 million Jews, millions of Soviet citizens and prisoners of war, millions of Polish and Yugoslav civilians, at least 70,000 men,
women and children with mental and physical handicaps, over 200,000
Gypsies, and unknown numbers of political prisoners, resistance fighters,
deportees and homosexuals (Bresheeth *et al.* 2000: 3). These figures are
approximate; in other texts it is noted that estimates, for example, of the
numbers of Gypsies killed ranges between 0.5 million to over 1 million (Gregory 2000a: 43). There is disagreement among those who argue the Holocaust is unique over the bases of this belief. The statistics are not the issue,
however; those who argue the Holocaust is unique no longer tend to do so on
numerical grounds: there is evidence suggesting greater numbers of people

were victims of the atrocities in Stalinist Russia and Mao's China compared with the Holocaust. For the proponents of the uniqueness argument, it is not the number of victims that makes the Holocaust unique, but that the killing was underpinned by an unbending anti-Semitic ideology:

> The Holocaust is phenomenologically unique by virtue of the fact that never before has a state set out, as a matter of intentional principle and actualized policy, to annihilate physically every man, woman, and child belonging to a specific people.
> (Katz 1996: 19)

Introducing the Holocaust presents the Holocaust as an example of genocide. Other examples cited include the case of the Native Americans, the Armenian massacres and 'ethnic cleansing' in former Yugoslavia. Similarly, Seymour Drescher presents parallels between the Holocaust and the Atlantic Slave Trade (Drescher 1996) and Robert F. Melson argues the Holocaust and the Armenian massacres are comparative histories (Melson 1996). To argue, as American scholar Steven T. Katz has done, that the Holocaust is unique on ideological grounds demands that the Holocaust be interpreted not only as incomparable but also as a uniquely Jewish experience. According to Katz, 'A close study of the relevant comparative historical data will show that only in the case of Jewry under the Third Reich was such all-inclusive, noncompromising, unmitigated murder intended' (Katz 1996: 20).

Katz refutes interpretations of the Holocaust that allow for comparisons to be drawn with other mass killings:

> I know of no method or technique that would allow one to weigh up, to quantify and compare, such massive evil and suffering, and I therefore avoid altogether this sort of counterproductive argument about what one might describe as comparative suffering.
> (Katz 1996: 19)

Deborah Lipstadt refers to comparative histories as 'immoral equivalencies' (Lipstadt 1994: 212). She argues against Ernst Nolte's suggestion that the Nazis borrowed their methods from Stalin (Nolte 1988) setting out the 'crucial contrasts' between the two dictators:

> Whereas Stalin's terror was arbitrary, Hitler's was targeted at a particular group ... The fate of every Jew who came under German rule was

essentially sealed. In contrast, no citizen of the Soviet Union assumed that deportation and death were inevitable consequences of his or her ethnic origins.
(Lipstadt 1994: 212)

Kinloch has taken issue with Lipstadt's argument:

It seems at least possible that inhabitants of the central Asian Soviet republic of Kazakhstan, for example, might have regarded the forcible imposition of collectivization on nomads, with its resultant famine, as a deliberate and murderous assault upon their ethnicity.
(Kinloch 2001: 11)

Similarly, the Rwandan genocide saw the ruthless pursuit of Tutsi families and anyone who protected them: 'The massacres are systematic in nature, whole families are exterminated – grandparents, parents and children. No one escapes, not even newborn babies . . . the victims are pursued to their very last refuge and killed there' (UN Special Rapporteur of the Commission on Human Rights, 25 May 1994, <http://www.rwandafund.org/sections/about/genocide.htm>).

Michael Marrus and Raul Hilberg also refuse to accept the Holocaust as unique. In *The Holocaust in History*, Marrus suggests the term 'unprecedented' is more useful than 'unique', writing that:

No event occurs without antecedents, and few would assert that there were no preceding instances of massacre or anti-Jewish persecution that bear a relationship to the murder of European Jewry. The real question is: how much of a break with the past is this particular event?
(Marrus 1987: 20)

However, there are historians and educationalists who would argue that there are at least elements of the Holocaust that are unique, if not in terms of scale or on ideological grounds, then in terms of the industrial method and planning behind the killing. Zygmunt Bauman argues the Holocaust is a unique modern genocide (1989), James M. Glass (1997) discusses the use of technology in the mass murder of the Jews. But speed cannot be the Holocaust's claim to uniqueness: Philip Gourevitch, in his book about the Rwandan genocide, *We Wish to Inform You that Tomorrow We Will Be Killed with Our Families*, writes that the rate of killing was three times that of the extermination of the Jews during the Holocaust after the Nazis had resorted to the gas chambers to speed up their killing (Gourevitch 1999).[4] And, as Stannard notes, in terms of technology, the dropping of the atomic bomb resulted in the deaths of 200,000 innocent Japanese civilians in a single nuclear instant (1996: 172). Phillip Lopate is not convinced that the speed or technology involved in the killing is important:

> Does it really matter so much if millions are gassed according to Eichmann's timetables, rather than slowly, crudely starved to death as in Stalin's regime, or marched around by ragged teenage Khmer Rouge soldiers and then beheaded or clubbed? Does the family mourning the loved one hacked to pieces by a spontaneous mob of Indonesian vigilantes care that much about the abuses of science and technology? Does neatness count, finally, so damn much?
> (Lopate 1989: 292)

Is it possible to study unique events?

Before discussing some of the reasons it might matter so much that the Holocaust is understood as unique, this chapter briefly outlines some of the problems for historians in such a claim. Understanding any event as unique impacts upon the study of history as Rogers explains: 'If events really were *unique* – each utterly unlike every other in all important respects – the whole process of understanding and explaining by analogy would be impossible. But this would abolish the possibility of historical explanation altogether' (Rogers 1984: 24).

Rogers' point is supported by Elton: 'the unique event is a freak and a frustration; if it is really unique – can never recur in meaning or implication – it lacks every measurable dimension and cannot be assessed' (Elton 1967: 11). If the cry of 'Never Again' is to have any substance, the Holocaust must be understood as comparable and comprehensible. Rather than arguing the Holocaust is unique, Gregory asserts that 'the Holocaust is surely the most important single event of the twentieth century' (Gregory 2000b: 52). It seems impossible as an historian to judge one event to be more important than another. This is particularly so if by making such a claim special status is conferred upon that event, as Elie Kedourie puts it:

> Just as no event is coherent or intelligible except in the context of other events, so no event can be specially privileged by the historian as being the sole key to, or the crucial explanation of, history or some stretch thereof. Some such implication, among many others, is to be derived from Ranke's famous statements that every epoch is directly before God

and that before God all generations of mankind are equal. This must be so, since the historian *qua* historian does not dispose of a standard or measuring rod, independent from and external to the events, which might enable him to declare one epoch more crucial, or one generation more important, than another.
(Kedourie 1984: 184–5)

It can be argued that historical events must be viewed in context, as part of a continuum, if they are to make sense. Sarah Rees Jones sees the Holocaust as part of a history of anti-Semitism: a deep-rooted pan-European prejudice without which 'twentieth-century anti-Semitism could not have taken the form it did' (Rees Jones 2000: 22).[5] At the Jewish Museum in Berlin, Daniel Libeskinds' building and the exhibition it houses depict the Holocaust as cutting across Jewish life and culture as two millennia of German-Jewish history is explored. In the words of W. Michael Blumenthal, it is:

In depicting the ups and downs of the relationship between Jews and non-Jews in Germany, the museum illustrates what becomes possible when religious, cultural or ethnic minorities are able to contribute their unique talents to national life and how terrible the consequences are for all when intolerance and prejudice prevail.
(Blumenthal 2001)

Such a presentation of the Holocaust allows lessons to be drawn for future generations in a way that could not be achieved if the Holocaust was understood as unique and incomparable. In an interview with Erna Paris, Hilberg made clear the point that lessons cannot be learned from the Holocaust if it is understood as unique:

For me the Holocaust was a vast, single event, but I am never going to use the word *unique* because I recognize that when one starts breaking it to pieces, which is my trade, one finds completely recognizable, ordinary ingredients that are common to other situations, such as Rwanda or Cambodia and possibly many others I have not examined. In the final analysis, it depends whether we want to emphasize the commonality with other events, or the holistic totality – in which case the Holocaust stands by itself. But I consider the latter perilous. Do we want one Rwanda after the other? You know, when a group of Tutsis sits around and watches a neighbouring village burn, when they say, 'well, that's them, it's not going to happen to us,' they are repeating the history of the Dutch Jews who, when they heard about the Holocaust in Poland, said, 'this is the

Netherlands; it can never happen here.' They are also repeating the words of the Germans in 1096 when they heard what the crusaders were doing in France. It is staggering to draw that line through the centuries and look at the sameness of language. You have to say, 'wait a minute, what's going on? Should we not look at this? Of course we should.' The alternative is to see the Holocaust as outside of history, as not part of anything. And it is impossible to learn from something that is so apart.
(Paris 2002: 335, emphasis in the original)

Hilberg talks in this quotation about drawing a line through history and paralleling the Holocaust with similar atrocities from history in order to really understand what the causal factors of genocide are. However, according to Lipstadt's thesis, attempts to compare the Holocaust to other mass killings are designed to help Germans come to terms with their past; she believes comparative histories imply Germany's actions were no worse than those of other countries. In Lipstadt's view, this is not far removed from the aims and methods of Holocaust deniers:

Intent on rewriting the annals of Germany's recent past, both groups [comparative historians and Holocaust deniers] wish to lift the burden of guilt they claim has been imposed on Germans. Both believe that the allies should bear a greater share of responsibility for the wrongs committed during the war. Both argue that the Holocaust has been unjustifiably singled out as a unique atrocity.
(Lipstadt 1994: 209)

Lipstadt sees denial as a spectrum on which comparative historians and neo-Nazis feature. She labels those who acknowledge the Holocaust as an appalling act of genocide but question the uniqueness of the *Jewish* experience as relativists or 'not yet deniers' (Lipstadt 1994: 215). Stannard condemns Lipstadt's work as 'intellectual thuggery' (Stannard 1996: 168). There are several points to be made about Lipstadt's thesis. First, there are circumstances, such as in this chapter, when the uniqueness of the Holocaust is legitimately discussed and questioned. Second, in view of the difficulties I encountered in the classroom with regard to attitudes towards Germans, Jews and refugees, Lipstadt's argument is worrying and possibly, in Stannard's words, 'violence provoking' (Stannard 1996: 167).

The German Ambassador Thomas Matussek has spoken about the teaching of Nazi Germany in British schools which he has claimed fuels xenophobia. The following comments followed an attack on two German schoolboys in London in 2002:

I want to see a more modern History Curriculum in schools . . . I think it very important that people know as much as possible about the Nazi period and the Holocaust. But what is equally important is the history of Germany in the past 45 years and the success story of modern German democracy. This is necessary to convey to young people that the Germans have learned their lesson and that they have changed.
(*The Guardian*, 9 December 2002)

Three years later, the Ambassador had the same message:

Whenever you talk with young Britons about Germany, or whenever you open the newspaper after a soccer game, you find immediately that you are immersed in the darkest chapter of German history: the Nazi period; the War; the Holocaust. And I think it is very, very good that people study it thoroughly. But it should not stop in 1945. It should also show a new, a modern, a democratic Germany, a Germany that has learnt its lessons.
(*Today*, 9 May 2005)

According to the Ambassador, most people in England asked to name a famous German, say 'Hitler'; they know little of modern Germany or German history other than the Nazi period (*Today*, 9 May 2005). History is a subject which has the potential to break down stereotypes and to promote tolerance, but it can also encourage racism and prejudice.

Is the claim for uniqueness 'a fearful plea for remembrance' (Rosenbaum 1998: 2)?

In recent years, Europe has witnessed a rise in support for the Far Right. In April 2002, Jean-Marie Le Pen became the first extreme right-wing candidate to get through to the second round of the French presidential elections, winning over 20 per cent of the vote. Then on 6 May that year, the Dutch right-wing politician, Pim Fortuyn, was shot dead. Fortuyn had been expected to do well in the General Election due to be held nine days after his death; he had been campaigning on an anti-immigration ticket. In the local elections held in England in May 2003, the British National Party (BNP) won seven seats to become the second largest party on Burnley Council. The Leader of the BNP, Nick Griffin, has announced himself as a Holocaust denier and, in a 1997 booklet entitled *Who are the Mind Benders?*, outlined a Jewish conspiracy to brainwash the British people in their own 'homeland' (<http://news.bbc.co.uk/1/hi/uk/1412785.stm>). Holocaust deniers claim that the Holocaust never occurred; the Jews made it up. Deniers dispute the minutiae and details of the Holocaust, such as the workings of the gas chambers and the number of Jews killed, in order to claim there was no policy to exterminate Jews during the Second World War. Holocaust denial appears to be motivated by anti-Semitism as well as by the presentation of a political ideology that promotes or attempts to excuse or condone fascism.

The issues of denial and uniqueness seem to be connected. In her first chapter, Lipstadt refers to the attempts of individuals to deny the Holocaust and says that, 'as time passes and fewer people can challenge these assertions, their campaign will only grow in intensity' (Lipstadt 1994: 3). Lipstadt shows concern for the future of Holocaust education:

> Colleagues have related that their students' questions are increasingly informed by Holocaust denial: 'How do we know that there really were gas chambers?' 'What proof do we have that the survivors are telling the truth?' 'Are we going to hear from the German side?' This unconscious incorporation of the deniers' argument into the students' thinking is particularly troublesome. It is an indication of the deniers' success in shaping the way coming generations will approach the study of the Holocaust.
> (Lipstadt 1994: 4)

These quotations are examples from Lipstadt's work that show concern for the future and the impact the claims of Holocaust deniers may have when there are no survivors left to discuss their experiences. Is the desire to attribute unique status to the Holocaust concerned to ensure that the Holocaust is remembered and to that end has a secure place on the school curriculum?

Brown and Davies, in some research based on teachers' perceptions of the Holocaust, identified four issues for further investigation. One of these was the fact that teachers may not perceive the Holocaust as being significantly unique (Brown and Davies 1998). According to Brown and Davies, teachers appeared to view the Holocaust as unique in the sense that all historical events are unique; they saw it as providing an opportunity to learn about 'the nature of humanity and human beings'. One teacher explained that in teaching the Holocaust a 'broader role which [assists the] growth of tolerance' is performed. A variety of other topics were mentioned by history teachers which were noted for the role they played in encouraging a more tolerant and democratic society. These topics included the actions of William the Conqueror following the Invasion in 1066; the massacre at Drogheda; the clearing of the Scottish Highlands; slavery; living conditions in

19th-century urban centres; the Vietnam War; and the wars in the former Yugoslavia and Rwanda (Brown and Davies 1998: 79). This view of the Holocaust within the History Curriculum is reminiscent of that put forward by Paula Mountford who uses lessons on the Holocaust to 'encourage pupils to recognize the relevance of a past event to today's world' (Mountford 2001: 28). In the first lesson in the sequence, Mountford begins with students deconstructing recent newspaper stories and identifying themes such as racism and physical violence. Students then make links between these themes and other topics they have studied in Years 7–9. Lessons on topics such as slavery, the suffragettes, the peasants' revolt, and the Luddites are recalled. The problem for Brown and Davies with such an approach is that 'the Holocaust becomes simply one of very many events which could be used as a tool to teach about tolerance' (Brown and Davies 1998: 79).

However, in his recent defence of Holocaust education for social and moral purposes, Short has advocated this kind of approach and recognized the need for teachers to be convinced of the importance of teaching the Holocaust to ensure the topic receives curriculum time:

> Debating the wider merits of the subject is not just a matter of theoretical interest, for the way the Holocaust is perceived is likely to influence the way it is taught and will almost certainly have a bearing on the amount of attention it receives. The historical significance of the Holocaust may not, therefore, be the only factor determining its status in the curriculum. If teachers believe the subject to be devoid of useful lessons, they might, quite reasonably, demand that it be given a more restricted role in students' education; after all, space on the curriculum is both highly prized and in short supply.
> (Short 2003b: 277)

Brown and Davies, who are similarly concerned that the Holocaust be taught in schools, would seem wary of such an approach but endorse the view that teachers need to be convinced of the importance of the Holocaust in order that the topic remains part of the school curriculum. They write that teaching the Holocaust for broader educational goals such as the growth of tolerance and learning about the nature of humanity:

> has a powerful attraction and would *seem* to lead to a situation in which the place of teaching and learning about the Holocaust is secure. However, if the Holocaust is not perceived as unique in a more significant way than any other historical event and, in the main, it is seen only as an example, then the motivation to teach it may be weakened.
> (Brown and Davies 1998: 79, emphasis in the original)

For Brown and Davies, the place of the Holocaust in the National Curriculum is important. In their view, the unique status conferred upon the Holocaust will ensure it remains central to the History Curriculum. However, the paragraphs above have demonstrated that there are questions regarding whether the Holocaust can be described as unique. Perhaps even more significant is the issue of whether anything can be learned from the Holocaust if it is perceived as unique. Indeed, in the above quotation, Short makes the point that the historical significance of the Holocaust may not be enough to ensure that history teachers teach about the Holocaust.

For history teachers teaching the topic of the Holocaust, the lack of a clear rationale for teaching the Holocaust in school history is compounded by the lack of consensus regarding the basic assumptions that underpin the teaching of this topic. This chapter has established that the related issues of terminology and uniqueness have been well debated in academia; though on the evidence of Chapter 1 this is not necessarily the case for history teachers. Only Anne highlighted and discussed definitions of the words 'Holocaust' and 'genocide'.

The desire to attribute unique status to the Holocaust appears to be concerned with ensuring its memory and, to that end, ensuring the position of the Holocaust in the school curriculum. But, as has been shown in this chapter, the view that if the Holocaust is perceived as unique then the status of the topic in the National Curriculum for History will be assured and unquestionable, is questionable. Perhaps the best way of guaranteeing the teaching of the Holocaust in school history may be to ensure history teachers have the opportunity to reflect on their teaching and debate for themselves the issues surrounding teaching the Holocaust.

Chapter 3

Teaching the Holocaust before 1991

This chapter looks at the history of the Holocaust as a topic for study in the secondary-school curriculum. It outlines the work of the Inner London Education Authority (ILEA) as well as efforts by Yad Vashem and the HET to encourage teachers to teach the Holocaust. The announcement that a national curriculum was to be introduced in England and Wales was made in 1986. Having discussed the attempts by the ILEA, Yad Vashem and the HET to establish the teaching of the Holocaust, this chapter goes on to outline the development of the National Curriculum for History, which became statutory in 1991.

The ILEA and the teaching of the Holocaust

Efforts to establish the teaching of the Holocaust in schools in England gathered momentum from the early 1980s. In 1983, the ILEA organized an exhibition about the Holocaust in the East End of London. Paul Flather wrote in the *Times Educational Supplement*, 'the exhibition will include items never before seen in Britain. It should be a major event, and a useful opportunity to teach a difficult subject'. The exhibition was accompanied by a teacher's pack, *Auschwitz: Yesterday's Racism*, which Flather described as 'extremely useful' (*TES*, 7 January 1983). This was one of a number of resources produced by the ILEA to support teachers teaching about the Holocaust.

The ILEA had its own audio-visual production unit based in Battersea and in 1985 produced two videos designed to help teachers with classroom discussions about the Holocaust. The first was 39 minutes in duration and intended for use with students aged 13. It was based on the 1983 exhibition and included historical film footage as well as photographs and drawings from Auschwitz State Museum in Poland. One history teacher in London who I spoke to during the course of the research continues to use this video in her teaching; she commented, 'even though the video is very old, it's fantastic'. The work of the ILEA in this area was pioneering.

The second video began with a 30-minute talk, given by Clive Lawton, then Education Director of the Board of Deputies of British Jews, and was aimed at teachers. In his lecture, Lawton addressed the dilemmas of teaching the Holocaust. Prior to the introduction of the National Curriculum in England, if teachers were going to teach about the Holocaust they had to be convinced of the importance of this topic since it was they who made the decisions about what they taught. Lawton opened his lecture with the statement, 'There's not a lot of point about talking about how to teach the Holocaust until we talk about whether to teach the Holocaust.' He continued, 'There are many, many teachers around the country who are worried about that particular problem.' Having outlined why he felt it was important to teach about the Holocaust, and discussed what he believed the term 'Holocaust' encompassed, Lawton moved on to discuss the possible pitfalls involved in teaching the Holocaust and suggested ways that some of these might be avoided. For example, Lawton warned, 'I think you have to watch the easy temptation of German-bashing.' He continued:

> One of the things that has to be established is the fact that this particular experience of the Holocaust was possible by compliance at least, and co-operation by many, acquiescence by a vast number and up to a point could have happened anywhere. We have within ourselves the potential to be involved in something like this and I think unless one explores and explores that, then again you are merely looking at an interesting incident of history and not looking at something more universally significant. So one of the ways of avoiding – if you like – German bashing, is to look at the fact of participation by other countries in the Holocaust either by activity or acquiescence ... The indifference to a considerable extent of the Allies deserves some mention. It's not all 'we're good, they're bad'. We know about the possibility of bombing the railroad into Auschwitz and the reluctance to do so because there were more important things to do. There was a war to fight.
> (ILEA 1985)

The teaching of the Holocaust does not, in my experience, reflect this perspective. Yet bearing in mind the perspective of the German Ambassador outlined in the previous chapter, it would seem prudent if it did. Further, if the Holocaust is to be taught as genocide prevention, students should surely be made aware of the wider picture and how the Holocaust was able to happen. Lawton's lecture encouraged teachers to think about teaching the Holocaust. He also emphasized the importance of having a clear rationale:

You cannot cover the whole subject. You have to find ways into the subject that are going to project the essential issues of what you might want to teach about the Holocaust. I am going to pose some. I'm not suggesting for one minute there is one ideal way of teaching the Holocaust and this is it. I'm just going to propose some and trigger some thinking.
(ILEA 1985)

In his lecture, Lawton encouraged teachers to consider what the term 'Holocaust' encompassed, and what their objectives were, before teaching about the Holocaust. He did not tell teachers how to teach the Holocaust, but encouraged *them* to think about this.[1]

A pack of resource material was published along with these videos. In an article for the *Jewish Chronicle* about these resources, Barrie Stead, Chairperson of the ILEA Schools Committee, wrote that the teachers' notes included a section which sought to stimulate teachers' ideas for discussion on how people behave when confronted by a phenomenon such as the Holocaust and went on to suggest some contemporary events that gave rise to the same issues of principle. He wrote:

To what extent, for example, are we aware of injustice, prejudice, discrimination, persecution in the world, in Europe, Britain, our own locality, in the playground? What do we do about those injustices? At what point is the line crossed from separate incidents and attitudes to what could be seen as 'State repression'?
(Stead 1986)

It was recommended in the notes that teachers look at the activities of groups such as Amnesty International and the Anti-Apartheid Movement and critically examine legislation such as the Official Secrets Act and the Police and Criminal Evidence Bill. This material acted as a prompt to Baroness Cox, then Conservative Education spokesperson, who initiated a debate in the House of Lords on the avoidance of politicization in education:

But perhaps even more disturbing is some of the material produced specifically on racism such as ILEA's teaching pack called *Auschwitz: Yesterday's Racism*. Much of this pack illustrates effectively the horrors of Auschwitz. That is unexceptionable. But education becomes political indoctrination when loaded questions and foregone conclusions are slipped in among the horrors of the death camp. For example, the teachers' guide suggests that children should make links today by comparing

Auschwitz with recent anti-trade-union legislation. Note the prefix 'anti' as an example of a typical foregone conclusion! The children are also to link Auschwitz with the behaviour of our police on picket lines and with the GCHQ issue.[2] I am not alone in finding this association of ideas and the trivialization of the horrors of Auschwitz particularly offensive. (Hansard, H. of L., Vol. 407, Col. 1141, 5 February 1986)

In his article, which answered critics of the ILEA's teaching materials on the Holocaust, Stead wrote:

Lady Cox claims that to link the Holocaust with contemporary social issues trivializes it. On the contrary, it would be more offensive to the memory of the millions who died to treat it as a finite historical phenomenon, a freak event with no significance for ourselves. (Stead 1986)

According to Stead, Lady Cox had described the main teaching pack *Auschwitz: Yesterday's Racism,* as dealing 'with the horrors of Auschwitz very sensitively' (Stead 1986). Perhaps Lady Cox's principle concern lay not with issues surrounding how the Holocaust should be understood and taught, but the impression young people (who were future voters) may gain in the classroom about the Conservative Government's policies and practice.[3] Such concerns would later lead Education Secretary Ken Clarke to introduce a '20-year rule'. He decided that in order 'to draw some sort of distinction between the study of history and the study of current affairs' (DES 1991) no event from the previous 20 years would be taught in the history classroom. This decision meant that 'the building of the Berlin Wall is history; its destruction is not' (Nash 1991). Clarke's '20-year rule' prevented history teachers from making links between history and current affairs, implied a distrust of history teachers and seemed to question their professionalism. It would appear that Clarke's mistrust of teachers was also experienced by Baroness Cox who had, on 9 October 1985, been quoted in the *Daily Telegraph* calling on Keith Joseph, then Secretary of State for Education, 'to issue clear guidelines for schools aimed at keeping politics out of the classroom'. However, as Lord McIntosh of Haringey explained in the debate in the House of Lords, the teaching material produced by the ILEA had been praised in the press and had the approval of the Board of Deputies of British Jews:

The noble Baroness referred to the ILEA material on Auschwitz and after. She has done so in public before. When she did so the last time

she was informed in a letter from the education officer to ILEA that the material had not only been prepared in conjunction with the Board of Deputies of British Jews but had been praised by the *Daily Telegraph* in July last year as being excellent teaching material.
(Hansard, H. of L., Vol. 407, Col 1171, 5 February 1986)

This debate is interesting. It highlights two different perspectives on the teaching of the Holocaust. While Baroness Cox saw the Holocaust as being historically important, the materials produced by the ILEA were designed not only to present the facts about Auschwitz, but also to encourage reflection on universal aspects of the Holocaust. The ILEA produced materials that would encourage and support teachers to teach about the Holocaust so that students would have the opportunity to learn about this event and to discuss issues arising from it which remained relevant. The ILEA were not advising that the Holocaust be taught exclusively in and as history. This book does not contend that there are not universal lessons to be learned that relate to the Holocaust, but that history teachers are tending to do the job of religious education or citizenship teachers, and students are being denied the opportunity to learn about the history of the Holocaust. This is the principal issue which this book aims to highlight and discuss.

Teaching the Holocaust: the report of a survey in the United Kingdom (1987)

Interestingly, while the ILEA was encouraging the teaching of the Holocaust in the school curriculum generally, there was an attempt in 1987 to audit how widely the Holocaust was being taught specifically in *history*. The Yad Vashem Charitable Trust[4] Education Sub-Committee wanted to find out to what extent the Holocaust was taught and examined in history in schools and further and higher education, with the ultimate aim of establishing the Holocaust as an *historical* topic for study. The *Report on the 1987 survey of United Kingdom Teaching on 'The Holocaust' or 'Nazi final solution to the Jewish question' and related subjects* was written by Fox and published in September 1989. The previous chapter reflected on terminology and highlighted Fox's misgivings regarding the term 'Holocaust'. It would appear from the title of this Report that the term 'Holocaust' was used in this survey to describe the Jewish experience, and the phrase 'and related subjects' to refer to the experience of 'others' who were persecuted because they did not fit into the Third Reich's regime.

The Yad Vashem Education Sub-Committee[5] designed four questionnaires: one for university and polytechnic departments of history and of education along with colleges of further and higher education; a second for local
education authorities (LEAs); the third category was local examination
boards; and the fourth sixth-form colleges and a selection of public/indepen-
dent schools. These questionnaires aimed to yield information in response to
six key questions:

Was the Holocaust or Nazi Final Solution of the Jewish Question and
related subjects being taught at educational institutions in Britain?

If so, was it being taught as a special study subject of its own, or as part of
other courses?

What were the nature of the courses in which it was taught? If it was
taught, specifically or incidentally, what was the age group of those learning the subject?

Was the subject represented in public examinations, particularly at
Advanced Level of General Certificate of Education, the old General
Certificate of Education Ordinary Level and the (then incoming) Gen-
eral Certificate of Secondary Education?

How interested were students and teaching staff in this particular subject?
(Fox 1989: 4)

In total, 506 questionnaires were sent out to educational establishments
across the United Kingdom. The Report provides an insight into the teaching of the Holocaust in history prior to the introduction of the National
Curriculum in 1991. Given the number of institutions involved in this
survey, a decision was made to send questionnaires to LEAs requesting
information about schools in their districts. This category is of the most
interest, and as can be seen from Table 3.1, it is also the category that
received fewer returns.

There were 57 LEAs which made no response at all while 15 wrote to say
that they lacked the time and resources to complete the questionnaire. Some
general information can be gleaned from this survey: of the 50 LEAs that did
return a complete questionnaire, 47 said that schools in their districts did
cover the Holocaust in either specific or general courses. In six cases, these
courses were taught to 11–16-year-olds, in 20 cases to 13–16-year-olds and
in 25 cases to 16–18-year-olds. From the returns from sixth-form colleges
and public/independent schools there is evidence that students were being

Table 3.1 Percentage returns of questionnaires sent out by the Yad Vashem Educational Sub-Committee.

Recipient	Number sent	Number return	% Return
i) Universities	55	40	72.7
Polytechnics	30	24	80.0
Univ./Poly. depts of education, colleges of further/higher education	128	43	33.6
ii) Local Education Authorities	122	50	41.0
iii) Local Examination Boards	8	7	87.5
iv) Sixth-form colleges	75	42	56.0
Public/independent Schools	88	43	48.9
TOTALS	506	249	49.2

(Fox 1989: 7)

taught about the Holocaust and were sitting public examinations on this topic. In addition, nearly half of the returns from the public/independent schools indicated that students aged 13 and above were learning about the Holocaust.

The Report stated that over the previous decade there had been an explosion in academic work relating to the Holocaust that would support serious historical study of this subject:

> Much as 'special subjects' like the Origins of the First or Second World Wars have their own methodology, documentation, bibliography, and advocates of differing schools of thought leading to constant debate (and enrichment) on the subject, so it is with the Holocaust and related subjects. (Fox 1989: 14)

The Yad Vashem Education Sub-Committee, via their survey and this Report, were calling for a greater commitment from educational institutions to a rigorous *historical* study of the Holocaust. While acknowledging the work being done in schools by teachers in departments such as religious education, it was argued that history was the rightful and logical home of Holocaust studies. More history was being researched and published in this area, and according to this Report, history teachers were abdicating their responsibility to this history:

> While it was realized at the outset that many Departments of Religious Studies/Education at all levels of the British system of education include some aspects of the Holocaust in their teaching studies, we felt that the main burden of this particular enquiry should be directed at Departments of History. This is because the intellectual discipline of history – obviously enough – should be the vanguard of the teaching process of this primarily historical subject.
> (Fox 1989: 5)

This survey was the first step in a campaign to establish the Holocaust as a subject for historical study in educational institutions. Wrote Antony Polonsky in his introduction to the Report:

> We believe, for a number of educational, historical, and moral reasons, that it is wrong to deny students of all ages a sufficient consideration in depth of one of the key historical events of this century, and one which has direct relevance on their present lives and future existence. It is our hope, therefore, that this Report will encourage a more positive attitude towards the Holocaust as a subject worthy of more educational time and attention in the United Kingdom.
> (Fox 1989: 3)

Fox stated in his conclusions and recommendations:

> As one of the university correspondents put it, they were unhappy with the questionnaire, since they felt it resaged a 'campaign' for more attention to be paid to the main subject in educational institutions in the United Kingdom. Actually he is quite right. But in such cases, there can be no 'campaign', no plans, no battle lines, until basic intelligence has first been obtained. After all, it could well have been the case that the intelligence thus obtained might have assured us all that the academic study of the Holocaust in the United Kingdom was healthy, widespread, intensive, academic, well researched, thoroughly informed, and highly productive in the way of published results. Of course it is not, and this was well known before the Survey was even attempted.
> (Fox 1989: 63)

However, if this Report was to form the basis of a campaign for a greater commitment to the teaching of the Holocaust in history then it was problematic. John Plowright, writing a response to the Report in *Teaching History* (1991), was critical of the approach that had been taken. He questioned why the study did not begin with 'first principles, such as establishing the importance of teaching the Holocaust and teaching it in a particular manner' (Plowright 1991: 26). As has been discussed in Chapter 2, the assumption that the Holocaust is a unique historical event is not universally agreed; Plowright argued that the case for the importance of teaching the Holocaust in history should be made to teachers, rather than relying on the assumed special status of the subject and demanding a place on the history curriculum on this basis. It was because the Report tended to assume the special status of the Holocaust, rather than setting out the basis of this belief, that Plowright believed it was 'seriously flawed' (1991: 27).

The Report itself did indicate that there was some debate about how the Holocaust should be taught:

> *Whilst many people believe that* a study of the history of European anti-Semitism is essential for understanding the origins of the Holocaust, *it is generally accepted that* the subject consists of three main parts: a) the study of Adolf Hitler and Nazi policies of persecution and extermination towards the Jews of Europe; b) an examination of the Jewish response in Germany and Europe to those Nazi policies; and c), an assessment of the non-Jewish response at government and non-government level, to Nazi policies towards the Jews.
> (Fox 1989: 14, emphasis added)

It is all the more surprising that the Report failed to establish 'first principles' given that Fox writes, 'two things emerge clearly from the results of the survey: suspicion as to its motives and purposes, and misunderstandings about the nature of academic study of the subject known generally as "the Holocaust" '. Fox goes on to note that 'at the present moment the subject of the Holocaust is very much a "Cinderella" one' (Fox 1989: 65), indicating the importance of teacher motivation.

Following the introduction of the National Curriculum, the importance of teacher motivation might have appeared to be less of an issue. The History Curriculum listed the Holocaust as compulsory. However, as was highlighted in Chapter 1, just because the topic of the Holocaust is compulsory does not mean that teachers are necessarily committed to teaching it. The importance of teacher motivation remains relevant. Also of continuing importance is, as Plowright highlighted, the establishment of 'first principles'. As the following chapter reveals, these have never been agreed.

The HET

In July 2001 I received a schools newsletter from the HET which boasted 'our first great success was to ensure the inclusion of the Holocaust on the new National Curriculum for History at Key Stage 3'. Interested by this statement I contacted the Trust in order to find out more about their early work.

The HET was born out of the work of an All Party Parliamentary War Crimes Group which was established in 1987 to look into allegations concerning Nazi war criminals and to make suggestions regarding possible legislation. The work of this group resulted in the 1991 War Crimes Act. The idea of a War Crimes Educational Trust (which would become known as the Holocaust Educational Trust) came out of a desire among the All Party Parliamentary War Crimes Group to educate the public in a period of renewed interest in Nazi war crimes and the Second World War.

The first meeting of the HET took place in the House of Commons on 25 January 1988. The Trust's Chairperson was Greville Janner QC. He was a Labour MP, former President of the Board of Deputies of British Jews, and served on the All Party Parliamentary War Crimes Group. Janner had begun making inquiries 8 months earlier into establishing an educational trust to disseminate resources and to provide training and research into 'the origin, nature, type and scope of war crimes; including the Holocaust – and related matters' (letter to Martin Paisner at Paisner and Co. (Solicitors) from Greville Janner, 12 May 1987).

By 16 November 1987, Janner was in a position to write to those who had agreed to serve on the HET with news that the Charity Commissioners had approved the HET, and he expected to receive a registered charity number by early December. The memorandum attached to Janner's letter named the Trustees: President, Lord Sainsbury; Chairperson, Greville Janner; Treasurer, Merlyn Rees (former Home Secretary); Joint Treasurer, John Wheeler (a Conservative MP); Trustee, Martin Paisner. The Board of Management included Sir Zelman Cowan, Martin Gilbert, Rabbi Hugo Gryn and Ben Helfgott. Cowan was Chairperson of the Press Council, Provost of Oriel College, Oxford and former Governor General of Australia. Gilbert was known as Churchill's biographer as well as for his academic work on the Holocaust. Gryn and Helfgott were both survivors of the Holocaust; in addition Helfgott was Chairperson of the Yad Vashem Committee of Board of Deputies. Philip Rubenstein, Secretary of the All Party Parliamentary War Crimes Group, was to become Director of the HET which was to 'take over all strictly charitable aspects of the work of the War Crimes Group – education in its broadest sense – including historical research' (Memorandum on the Holocaust Educational Trust from Greville Janner QC MP). Elie Wiesel was named as Patron of the Trust. Later the Rt Hon. Lord Jakobovits, His Grace the Duke of Norfolk and the Rt Revd Lord Runcie also gave their patronage. In a letter to Wiesel, Janner commented, 'the Holocaust Educational Trust ... has the most heavyweight representation there could possibly be' (letter to Elie Wiesel from Greville Janner, 30 November 1987).[6]

Janner's commitment to furthering Holocaust education is clear; there are examples of warlike imagery in his description of the Trustees as 'troops set for battle' and 'a powerful mob'. Janner was determined that there should be a greater awareness among the public about the Holocaust. In a letter to Wiesel written on 9 November 1987 he wrote:

> Your address was memorable and marvellous. It is also highly quotable and I am getting copies of the transcript, for distribution to our Parliamentary War Crimes Group. It will explain in a way that I cannot do why their work is of such lasting importance – and how that importance can grow, even as the Holocaust itself moves away in time ... It is appalling that there is no exhibition, no museum, no input into our educational system, to remind – and to fight against indifference.

One of the first activities of the newly formed HET was to produce an educational trigger video entitled *Telling the Story: Nazi War Criminals on Trial*, with accompanying notes for teachers. With the introduction of the War Crimes Act, ensuring the memory of the Holocaust was particularly important if the public were to be convinced it was right to put Nazi war criminals on trial despite the passage of time.

The HET also showed interest in Fox's Report; the author agreed to send a copy of the conclusion of this Report to the HET prior to its publication (letter to Dawn Waterman [at the HET] from John P. Fox, 25 February 1988). One of the Trust's main aims was to establish the teaching of the Holocaust in all schools. They listed their objectives as being:

- to promote research into the Holocaust;
- to assist with the work of individuals and organizations involved in Holocaust education;
- to promote the collection of archival materials and artefacts relating to the Holocaust period;
- to produce written and audio-visual materials on the subject of the Holocaust;
- to promote the teaching of the Holocaust in schools and colleges.

(HET document detailing the aims, individuals and major projects the Trust has been involved with)

Teaching the Holocaust at examination before 1991

In addition to the Fox Report, there is some further evidence of teaching the Holocaust at examination level prior to the introduction of the National Curriculum. During April 1988, Spartacus Educational Publishers sent out questionnaires to all history departments in Britain's secondary schools; the responses received provide a further indication of the extent to which Nazi Germany and the Holocaust may have been taught prior to the introduction of the National Curriculum. By the end of 1988, 460 history teachers from 387 schools had returned their questionnaires. The results of this survey indicated the growing preference for modern-world history at GCSE (the syllabus for modern-world history would in all likelihood cover Nazi Germany and the Holocaust): 48.83 per cent of the history departments who responded followed a syllabus in modern-world history, while 31.52 per cent taught British social and economic history since 1750, and 24.03 per cent taught the School History Project. Indeed, it was noted in the interim report produced by the History Working Group (HWG) that 'the history of modern Britain and Europe has modest popularity' (DES 1989: 8).

In May 1989, the Spiro Institute[7] held their first teachers' conference, staged in response to the growing number of schools teaching the Holocaust at GCSE and A level. The conference was designed to support teachers and to discuss approaches to teaching the Holocaust. In an article in the *Jewish Chronicle* reporting on the conference, under the headline 'Children Stunned by Holocaust Horror', Supple is quoted: 'you must make it [the Holocaust] mean something. You can get the kids thinking about their own lives and behaviour, like bullying and racism' (*Jewish Chronicle*, 19 May 1989). Supple taught history in Tyneside. She saw a serious and urgent need for materials concerning the Holocaust, feeling that current resources were limited and superficial or unsuitable for use with GCSE students. In 1988, Supple embarked on a GCSE topic book on the subject of the Holocaust for use not only in history, but across humanities subjects (*TES*, 13 May 1988). Landau, who was both a member of the Yad Vashem Educational Sub-Committee and Educational Director of the Spiro Institute, is quoted in an article in the *TES* which discussed Supple's project: 'every week I receive desperate calls from teachers who complain that they feel under-informed, under-resourced and generally unfit to cope with the enormity of this subject and its implications' (*TES*, 13 May 1988).

Plans to introduce a National Curriculum were announced by the then Education Secretary, Kenneth Baker,[8] on London Weekend Television's *Weekend World*, broadcast on 7 December 1986. The Fox Report, Spartacus Survey and increasing demand from teachers for support show that the Holocaust was being taught in school history before the introduction of the National Curriculum. Campaigners for the extension of Holocaust education, such as the HET, would be concerned that the new National Curriculum would support and extend this teaching and learning.

The Origins of the National Curriculum for History

The ERA passed in 1988 provided for the establishment of a national curriculum of core (maths, science, English) and foundation (technology, history, geography, modern foreign languages, art, music, physical education) subjects. For each subject there were objectives known as attainment targets for the knowledge, skills and understanding which students should be expected to have acquired by the end of the academic year in which they were aged 7, 11, 14 and 16. These were 'key ages' and, therefore, students aged between five and seven were in Key Stage 1, students aged seven to 11 were in Key Stage 2, students aged 11 to 14 were in Key Stage 3 and those aged 14 to 16 were in Key Stage 4. Programmes of study would also be drawn up to detail the content, skills and processes which would need to be covered during each key stage. The attainment targets and programmes of study would together form the basis of the standard attainment tasks (SATs) which would assess students at the end of each key stage (National Curriculum History Working Group Terms of Reference). Working groups were established to develop the attainment targets and programmes of study for each National Curriculum subject.

This conception of the National Curriculum was one of the reasons that Lawton and Chitty (1988), along with other commentators, believed the National Curriculum to be fundamentally flawed:

The curriculum is conceived of entirely in terms of subjects, with little or no acknowledgement of the debate which has been going on both inside and outside the DES for at least the last 10 years. Although largely educated and trained *within* subject disciplines, teachers have to learn to apply their knowledge and skills in ways which stretch far beyond single subjects and inevitably cross subject boundaries. They have to ask, as HMI [Her Majesty's Inspectorate] working groups have done, what are

the essential areas of learning and experience to which all children have a right of access.
(Lawton and Chitty 1988: 3–4)

This is an important issue that is of continuing relevance with regard to the topic of the Holocaust, which does not sit easily within any one subject boundary. This will be returned to in the concluding chapter.

Facts versus skills

A political battle has been raging over school history. At issue is the Conservative conviction that children should learn more facts, especially about British history.
(*Clean Slate Special*, 17 October 1990)

The new National Curriculum for History would also have to engage with and attempt to resolve some of the contemporary debates in history education.

In their book *Understanding History Teaching: teaching and learning about the past in secondary schools* (2003) Chris Husbands, Alison Kitson and Anna Pendry set out the two traditions which have shaped school history: the great tradition and the alternative tradition (Husbands *et al.* 2003: 7–14). These two traditions are clearly summarized and presented in Table 3.2 which has been taken from this text.

The alternative tradition developed during the 1960s and 1970s and challenged the great tradition of history teaching, although Husbands *et al.* note that the assumptions underpinning the great tradition have never been uncontested. But it was not until the establishment of the Schools' Council in 1963 that the great tradition came under sustained pressure (Husbands *et al.* 2003: 9). It was through the work of the Schools Council History Project (SCHP) that the alternative tradition, or 'new' history, came about. Their projects developed an approach to history teaching which broke away from traditional, academic methods and attempted to engage students in the process and study of history. Through use of active learning the aim was to make history relevant and interesting to students. According to Slater, it was 'the most significant and beneficial influence on the learning of history and the raising of its standards to emerge this century' (Slater 1989: 2). History was becoming more than a lesson in memory recall; empathy and cause were now considered by students who used primary sources as evidence. The work of theorists such as Coltham and Fines (1971) also

Table 3.2 The two traditions of history teaching

	The 'great tradition'	The alternative tradition
Learners and pedagogy	• Emphasizes the didactically active role of the teacher. • Assumes a high level of teacher subject knowledge. • Learner's role is largely passive.	• Emphasizes constructivist models of learner engagement with the past. • Places a premium on teacher's ability to manage student learning activities.
Content	• Characterized by a concern with national history. • Focuses on the understanding of the present through engagement with the past.	• Characterized by a variety of content reflecting world history and the experiences of a variety of groups. • Stresses the importance of learning about a variety of historical situations and contexts.
Purposes of learning history	• Defined through the content of the subject. • Focuses substantially on the cultural capital of historical content.	• Defined through the contribution of the subject to wider general education. • Focuses substantially on preparation for working life and the acquisition of skills.

(Husbands *et al.* 2003: 12)

helped to reconceptualize school history in these two decades. Coltham and Fines' work *Educational Objectives for the Study of History: a suggested framework* attempted to set out the skills that could be developed through history.

These developments in school history mirrored developments in academic history where, during the 1960s and 1970s, the grand narrative came under attack from so-called 'new histories'. At the same time as 'new histories' were being researched and published on the lives of, for example, the working-class poor (Thompson 1965) and women (Rowbotham 1973), assumptions about the content of the school history curriculum were similarly shifting to become more inclusive. As Husbands *et al.* note, 'the content base of history degrees shifted markedly in the 1960s and

1970s, with consequent implications for the knowledge and conceptual base of those graduates who subsequently became history teachers' (2003: 10).

According to Mary Price, changes in the approach to history teaching were very much needed. In 1968, she wrote that history was 'in danger'. Regarded by students as a 'useless and boring' subject she feared 'history could lose the battle not only for its place in the curriculum but for a place in the hearts and minds of the young'. Price felt that a series of factors contributed to the fact that history was 'losing the battle' to other subjects: history syllabuses were tired and narrow with a focus on British history; there was a notion that history was suitable only for more able students; and the teaching of history was didactic, relying on note-taking and rote-learning (Price 1968).

Speaking on BBC 2's *Clean Slate Special* in 1990, Carol White, a history teacher who served on the National Curriculum HWG, explained that concerns such as Price's were what was really behind 'new history':

> History was very much under threat in the 1950s and 1960s and children, when they had the choice, were voting with their feet by giving it up in droves. And if we had a look at how it was being taught, for many children the demands of memory recall and rote learning were such that if they didn't have a particularly good memory then the actual historical study was meaningless. Therefore, and this was what was behind the so-called new history – which is now distinctly middle aged – in fact we begin to have a look at what constitutes an understanding of what happened in the past in terms of what happened and why things happened. We did in fact discover children became far more interested and involved and I would argue, in the end, knew more.
> (*Clean Slate Special*, 17 October 1990)

By the time the Government announced the introduction of the National Curriculum, the great tradition of history teaching 'was under substantial attack from a quite different tradition of history teaching' (Husbands *et al.* 2003: 12). However, new history had not been universally adopted. There were criticisms of this approach. In order to complete in-depth studies, some content had to be sacrificed. Traditional teaching was also more successful in transmitting a sense of chronology to students. The introduction of the GCSE in 1988 polarized the debate as examination boards appeared to have been influenced by the proponents of new history. Wrote Beattie, 'whatever else it may be, history is not new' (1987: 24). He was critical of the approach not least because he saw it as giving rise to moral relativism which he viewed with contempt 'if God is not the examiner, how will such judgements [as a GCSE answer to the question, to what extent do you think that Germany was fairly treated by the terms of the Treaty of Versailles?] be assessed?' (Beattie 1987: 7). Beattie saw history as 'a detailed factual story'; moralizing, in his view, was not central to the role of the historian. He criticized attempts to make history more relevant to students:

> Emphasizing the importance of relevance of current events directs attention to areas (such as the present Middle Eastern situation) on which historical scholarship is necessarily silent. This turns history into 'politics' or 'current affairs', and the pretence of introducing pupils to historical enquiry is dropped: history is simply redefined as whatever is in today's newspapers.
> (Beattie 1987: 8)

Beattie's arguments were typical of the thinking of members of the so-called New Right.[9] This group contained proponents of the great tradition of history teaching, arguing for greater emphasis on British history in the school curriculum on the grounds of national identity, pride and common cultural values (Husbands *et al*. 2003: 121).

Just over a quarter of schools were following a Schools History Project syllabus as the debate about history in the National Curriculum erupted (Phillips 1998: 18). In England and Wales the formation of the National Curriculum for History saw fierce debate among educationalists, politicians and in the media. While vigorous debate took place in other subject areas, and particularly over the English curriculum, the level of political interest in the formation of the History Curriculum was not mirrored elsewhere. Not only were questions directly relating to the History Curriculum raised in the House of Commons, but leading politicians as well as the Prime Minister herself, became involved in the 'great history debate' (Phillips 1998).

The role of the HWG

The HWG was set up to advise the Secretary of State on the statutory framework for History. The Group met for the first time on 24 January 1989. The original group comprised ten members: Commdr Michael Saunders Watson (Chairperson), Mr Robert Guyver, Mr Jim Hendy, Mr Tom Hobhouse, Dr (now Professor) Gareth Elwyn Jones, Mr Peter Livsey, Mrs Ann Low-Beer, Dr Alice Prochaska, the late Dr John Roberts and Mrs Carol White. In addition, all of the National Curriculum working groups had an 'observer' from HMI and representatives from the DES also attended the HWG's meetings.

R. Phillips (1993: 54) notes the importance of knowing something about the characters who served on the HWG for establishing the likely direction this group would take. Michael Saunders Watson owned Rockingham Castle in Leicestershire and was Chairperson of the Heritage Education Trust; he shared with Baker an interest in history and heritage. In an interview for *The Independent* on 8 April 1990, Saunders Watson said he 'felt he'd been appointed by Baker because of the need to have somebody outside the academic world' and also, 'Baker had stayed at his house one night'. Blum has commented that Baker's decision to appoint Saunders Watson as Chairperson on this basis was dubious (Blum 1990). However, according to the HMI Observer, Saunders Watson quickly understood the current debates in history and education (interview, 20 June 2002). Indeed, Melanie Phillips in *All Must Have Prizes* described Saunders Watson's appointment as a 'spectacular own goal' (Phillips 1996: 148). But *if* Baker had wanted a 'lackey' he had made a mistake. Saunders Watson was determined that despite the level of political interest and attempts to apply pressure on the group, their work would be their own. He defended the decisions made by the HWG and argued the case against knowledge-based attainment targets, which was the favoured approach of Thatcher and the New Right (see below). As R. Phillips has written, Saunders Watson 'was hardly a left-wing subversive (but as it turned out he was not a Thatcherite either)' (Phillips 1998: 55).

Baker appointed just two teachers to the Group: Robert Guyver (a primary-school teacher and Chairperson of the Devon Association of Teachers of History) and Carol White (a secondary-school teacher who had expressed concerns about elements of the Schools History Project). Ann Low-Beer and Dr Gareth Elwyn Jones both worked in teacher education. Ann Low-Beer was a lecturer in education at Bristol University. She had also run short courses on history and the primary school for primary teachers, and had written articles critical of the use of empathy in history lessons (Low-Beer 1967, 1987, 1988, 1989). Gareth Elwyn Jones was based at the University of Wales, Swansea. His role was to link and co-ordinate the approaches of the HWG with the Group's Welsh counterpart, the History Committee for Wales. John Roberts was a high-profile academic historian and Warden of Merton College, Oxford. His commitment to Oxford meant that due to the demands on his time he resigned following the publication of the interim report. Professor Peter Marshall, who specialized in European history, replaced him. Marshall was Rhodes Professor at King's College, London. Alice Prochaska was Secretary and Librarian to the Institute of Historical Research at the University of London. She had also been a member of the History at the Universities Defence Group and, as such, realized that the presentation of school history was of importance if the subject was going to survive in universities. She had experience of working with academics and school teachers. Like Jones (1991) and Guyver (1990), Prochaska later wrote of her experiences on the HWG (1990). She had previously published *History of the General Federation of Trade Unions* (1982). Peter Livsey was a secondary-school adviser. Henry Hobhouse was author of *The Forces of Change: why we are the way we are now* (1989) in which he argued modern history has been shaped less by the actions of human beings than by three natural forces: population growth, food supply and disease. He had an interest in politics and served as the Conservative Chairperson on Somerset County Council between 1989 and 1992. Jim Hendy was Director of Education at Stockport Metropolitan Borough Council. Chris Culpin (author of school history textbooks) was co-opted onto the Group later (from 23 October 1989) as was Dr Tim Lomas (a history teacher with the reputation of being expert in the area of assessment, co-opted from 10 July 1989). From the DES, Michael Phipps, who was Head of the Schools Curriculum Policy Division concerned with arts and humanities, attended all but one meeting until 29 September when he was replaced by Barney Baker. Jenny Bacon, Head of Schools Branch 3, also attended some meetings until August 1989 when Anthony Chamier took over the post. Jenny Worsfold was responsible for producing the minutes, helping to draw up agendas and co-ordinating the work of the HWG and DES; she was assisted by Phil Snell,[10] Lesley Storey and John Goodwin.

Roger Hennessey was Staff Inspector for History and was invited to be HMI Observer to the HWG. However, according to the Group members, Hennessey did more than observe the Group's work: he influenced the decisions and thinking of the HWG and worked very closely with the Chairperson, and with the Secretary, Jenny Worsfold. Together, the three of them formed the 'management group'. Alice Prochaska (1990) reflected that Roger Hennessey and Jenny Worsfold were two of the most important people, despite not technically being members of the group. Of Hennessey she wrote, '[he] dedicated an enormous amount of his time to the task of advising us in his official capacity of "observer"' (Prochaska 1990: 83). An indication of Hennessey's views on school history can be found in *History from 5 to 16 Curriculum Matters 11* (DES 1988), an HMI document for which he was mainly responsible. This document featured on the list of background reading issued to the HWG in January 1989 (List of background reading for members of the HWG, January 1989).

It is worth digressing here to write something about this paper and Hennessey's thinking about school history, since these appear to have informed the Group's work. During the Group's second meeting, members of the HWG were told that comments on the HMI document were due at the end of February and although these might not be issued in published form, they would be made available to the Group (NC/HWG (89) 2nd). The preface to the HMI document made clear that its aim was to encourage professional debate:

> This paper is addressed not only to heads and teachers but also to school governors, local education authority elected members and officers, parents, employers and the wider community outside the school. Like other earlier publications in the Curriculum Matters series, this is a discussion paper intended to stimulate a professional debate and to contribute to reaching national agreement about the objectives and content of the school curriculum. The debate will now take place within the arrangements for developing the National Curriculum contained in the Education Reform Act.
> (DES 1988: iv)

Comments were invited from readers of the document, to be sent to the Staff Inspector for History by 28 February 1989. As noted by Chitty and Lawton in the quotation above, HMI working groups had been probing the question 'What are the essential areas of learning and experience to which all children have a right of access?' Hennessey viewed this as an important question and saw that it could, as noted in the preface to the HMI document, now be debated through the development of the National Curriculum, about which he was positive. In an article for *The Historian* in autumn 1988, Hennessey wrote, 'the National Curriculum offers all parties an unrepeatable opportunity. It is just possible that two major developments will coincide: the National Curriculum, and the "higher wisdom" which might arise from a synthesis of all the debating of the last decade' (1988). Hennessey believed that a major problem with the status quo prior to 1989 was that no one had ever sat down and considered what we, as a society, want our 16-year-olds to know and be able to do by the time they leave school. He further saw a role for the development of the National Curriculum for History in ending the skills and knowledge debate (see below) and putting a stop to those who said that history was irrelevant (interview, 26 June 2002).

The reasons for studying history and the aims of teaching history in schools outlined in the HMI document were a fusion of the traditional and modern approaches. This was similarly the case in the interim and final reports of the HWG. In their final report (DES 1990) the HWG referred to the debate over the nature and function of history, writing that:

> There exist many, often strongly held and divergent, opinions about school history. Even before the publication of our Interim Report we

were aware of this from our own experience, from the volume of corre-spondence received, and from meetings held with a range of people. We consider it neither desirable nor possible to search for a formula which could please everyone and drew up our proposals according to our terms of reference.

(DES 1990: 1)

The HWG listed the purposes of school history:

1   To help understand the present in the context of the past.
2   To arouse interest in the past.
3   To help give pupils a sense of identity.
4   To help give pupils a sense of their own cultural roots and shared inher-itances.
5   To contribute to pupils' knowledge and understanding of other coun-tries and other cultures in the modern world.
6   To train the mind by means of disciplined study.
7   To introduce pupils to the distinctive methodology of historians.
8   To enrich other areas of the curriculum.
9   To prepare pupils for adult life.

(DES 1989: 5–6; 1990: 1–2)

This list can be seen as a compromise between the great tradition and new history – and, indeed, the polemic argument between Carr (1961) and Elton (1967). Items 2, 4, 5, 8 and 9 are in line with new history, while Items 1, 3, 6 and 7 represent traditional viewpoints on the nature and pur-pose of history. Rather than resolving the debate and providing a clear rationale for school history, the National Curriculum 'was based around a policy of compromise which appeared to hold the two traditions in creative tension' (Husbands *et al.* 2003: 13). Thus, Husbands *et al.* write that 'there were those [teachers] firmly embedded at one extreme or another of each tradition, but most history teachers moved, in terms of their own practice, between the assumptions of the two traditions' (2003: 13).

   Also discussed in the HMI paper were issues surrounding the planning of history courses; some of the principles of teaching and learning history; and implications for the assessment of history. Assessment of history in the National Curriculum was a contentious issue. As has been noted, Thatcher and the New Right rejected 'new history' and believed that factual knowl-edge alone should be tested. However, the HWG saw knowledge and skills as interdependent and insisted that assessment be based on knowledge *and* understanding of historical concepts. This same view is put forward in the HMI paper:

A knowledge and understanding of past events, when they occurred and what might have been their causes and consequences, is certainly a necessary part of understanding history. But closely linked to a growing understanding of events of the past should be an increasing mastery of historical skills. These are inter-dependent activities which ought to develop together.

(DES 1988: 23)

Teachers' response to the establishment of the HWG

The response of the teaching profession to the establishment of the HWG was perhaps less positive than that of Hennessey. Three members of the Group who were interviewed were particularly aware of the general un-popularity of the proposed National Curriculum and the establishment of a working group hand-picked by the Government and closely supervised by civil servants. Prochaska wrote, 'the idea of being told what they [teachers] must teach was anathema' (1990: 80). One Group member told me that his brother accused him of being the mouthpiece of the establishment (inter-view, 2 April 2002). Both this member and two other members of the Group said that they agreed to serve on the HWG because of the conspira-tor's argument throughout history: if I do not do it, someone else will:

It [the National Curriculum] was very controversial, lots of people had said they would have nothing to do with it, they didn't want to be seen as Thatcher's poodles! My friends said I should do it because they thought I would be good at it (well, they were my friends) and if I didn't do it some-one else who might not be as good would do it.
(Interview, 29 July 2002)

Like Alice [Prochaska] writes in her article[11] you had this feeling, well if I don't do it then someone else will and they'll make a worse job of it. Which of course is nonsense and has been the collaborator's argument through-out history! [But] I felt it was the right thing to do.
(Interview, 24 June 2002)

The Group did not have a free hand: Terms of Reference

Baker wanted to see the Group's interim report by 30 June 1989. Their report was to indicate the contribution history should make to the school curriculum; their provisional thinking about the knowledge, skills, and understanding students should have acquired by the end of each key stage; and the Group's thinking about the programmes of study and attainment targets (National Curriculum History Working Group Terms of Reference). The Group did not have a free hand. In his supplementary guidance to the HWG, Baker made clear that the National Curriculum for History should have an emphasis on British history. He wrote that school history should 'help pupils come to understand how a free and democratic society has developed over the centuries' placing at its 'core the history of Britain, the record of its past and, in particular its political, constitutional and cultural heritage' (Supplementary Guidance to the HWG). This was reiterated by Baker when he visited the group during their first meeting at Elizabeth House in London. Baker was also concerned about the teaching of contemporary history. Despite agreeing that 'an international dimension was important to history, particularly in the twentieth century' he 'warned that this should not be achieved through making history into twentieth century studies' (NC/HWG (89) 1st). The issues of an emphasis on British history and the teaching of the late 20th century would be recurrent debates during the formation and revision of the National Curriculum for History.

The ideological importance of history

British history characterizes the Nation's image of itself. Change the history and you change the country's identity. For the 1990s the question is where that identity lies.
(*Clean Slate Special*, 17 October 1990)

Ideologically, history is a powerful subject which shapes national identity (Phillips *et al.* 1999). In her diary detailing her experiences as a member of the HWG, Prochaska wrote that 'history is of all the subjects most vulnerable to misuse for political reasons' (Prochaska 1990: 81). This point is supported by Sirkka Ahonen, who views school history in Estonia as invention, designed by politicians to support first the Communists and then the independent state of Estonia. Under Communism, Moscow controlled the framework for the school history curriculum. The content was intended to develop in students a sense of nationalism; the Soviet Union was their 'fatherland'. Estonia was viewed as 'an ethnic territory' and the proportion of curriculum time available to teach Estonian history was limited to 10 per cent. In 1991, Estonia gained independence, 'the new curriculum sought to empower the population to work hard for a new state' (Ahonen 2001: 183). Students were presented with a history of their country's inevitable development towards an independent nation-state. This interpretation of history excluded the minority of Russian-speaking Estonians comprising 36 per cent of the population; they were not part of the new Estonia, and their history was 'embedded in the story of the evil occupant, the Soviet Union' (Ahonen 2001: 183).

The HWG's interim report did not meet with the approval of the Prime Minister. She was 'appalled' (Thatcher 1993: 596) by the contents of the report. Thatcher wrote in her memoirs:

> It [the interim report] put emphasis on interpretation and enquiry as against content and knowledge. There was insufficient weight given to British history. There was not enough emphasis on history as chronological study. Ken Baker wanted to give the report a general welcome while urging its chairman [*sic*] to make the attainment targets specify more clearly factual knowledge and increasing the British history content. But this in my view did not go far enough. I considered the document comprehensively flawed and told Ken that there must be major, not just minor, changes. In particular, I wanted to see a clearly set out chronological framework for the whole History Curriculum. But the test would of course be the Final Report.
> (Thatcher 1993: 596)

The great tradition of history teaching saw history as a means of transmitting important messages about national identity based on notions of a shared cultural heritage and a progressive development of democracy (Husbands *et al.*, 2003: 116).

Thatcher believed firmly in the great tradition; she stressed the importance of students learning facts and dates. Indeed, the issue at the heart of the 'great history debate' (Phillips 1998) was the Conservatives' conviction that children should learn more facts, especially about 'British' history:

> History is an account of what happened in the past. Learning history, therefore, requires knowledge of events. It is impossible to make sense of such events without absorbing sufficient factual information and without being able to place matters in a clear chronological framework which means knowing dates.
> (Thatcher 1993: 595)

During Prime Minister's Question Time on 29 March 1990, John Stokes MP asked:

Is my right hon. Friend aware that there is considerable anxiety about the teaching of English history in our schools? Instead of teaching only what are called themes, why cannot we go back to the good old days when we learnt by heart the names of the kings and queens of England, the names of our warriors and battles and the glorious deeds of our past?

The Prime Minister replied that:

As usual, my hon. Friend is absolutely right. What children should be taught in history is the subject of vigorous debate. I agree with him. Most of us are expected to learn from experience of history and we cannot do that unless we know it. Children should know the great landmarks of British history and should be taught them at school.
(Hansard, H. of C., Vol. 170, Col 668, 29 March 1990)

It could be argued that history as perceived in this sense, without the procedural concepts such as historical evidence and explanation, may be better described as antiquarianism. Even if school history is about content alone, Thatcher's perception of the subject is perhaps questionable since history as a discipline is not static; it is constantly growing and developing. New historical evidence as well as different methodologies mean that our understanding and interpretation of historical events and personalities are revised. Landmarks and their meanings change. Kettle has suggested that for the Conservatives the debate surrounding the National Curriculum for History was not about what history is; he suggests that in fact they had realized that there was something much bigger at stake:

Margaret Thatcher has fought many historic battles for what she sees as Britain's future. Few of them, though, are as pregnant with meaning as her current battle for control over Britain's own history . . . The debate is a surrogate for a much wider debate about the cultural legacy of the Thatcher years. It is about the right to dissent and debate not just history but a range of other assumptions. If the Prime Minister can change the way we are taught history, she will have succeeded in changing the ground rules for a generation to come. It is a big prize.
(*The Guardian*, 4 January 1990)

Indeed, Crawford believed the purpose of the National Curriculum was:

to help produce a particular kind of society by using history education as a vehicle through which to disseminate a specific set of values and beliefs by attempts to control definitions of the past designed to help justify political action, promote particular social trends and develop economic doctrines. (Crawford 1995)

In a cabinet re-shuffle in July 1989 Baker was moved from Education to make way for John MacGregor who Thatcher believed 'would prove more effective in keeping a grip on education reforms' (Thatcher 1993: 596). The Prime Minister's resistance to the proposals outlined by the HWG in their interim report may explain MacGregor's insistence in his letter to Saunders Watson published with this document that the Group look again at 'a number of issues':

> We are publishing the Report today, together with this letter. I have set out below a number of issues which I would like the Group to consider further in developing complete and detailed recommendations for attainment targets, programmes of study and related assessment arrangements, for inclusion in its Final Report at Christmas. You will of course also be taking account of public reaction to the Interim Report, and I know that you will want to make sure that they can be easily implemented in schools. (Letter to Cmndr Michael Saunders Watson from John MacGregor published in DES 1989)

These 'issues' were chronology, the proportion of British history recommended and assessment. In terms of this thesis, the issue of British history is the most interesting. MacGregor noted that less than 50 per cent of the proposed history curriculum was made up of British history: 'I should like the group to increase this proportion by developing additional core study units devoted to British history and, in the appropriate thematic history study units, to give the British experience a sharper focus' (DES 1989). As will be discussed in the following chapter, it was within this statement that a cross-party group of MPs saw an opportunity to argue for the inclusion of the Second World War and the Holocaust in the National Curriculum for History.

This chapter demonstrates that in the years immediately prior to the 1988 ERA, efforts to establish the teaching of the Holocaust in schools in England gathered momentum. Interestingly, however, only the Yad Vashem Education Sub-Committee was campaigning for the Holocaust to receive greater time and attention in school history. Janner's thinking appears to have been about furthering Holocaust education more generally. In his letter to Wiesel, he stressed the importance of keeping alive the memory of what happened and expressed astonishment and upset at the lack of input into the education system. The introduction of the National Curriculum provided an opportunity for those concerned about Holocaust education to have legislation put in place to mandate the teaching of the topic. But as the following chapter reveals, there was a question of whether the Holocaust should be a compulsory topic in school history.

Chapter 4

The question of whether the Holocaust should be compulsory in school history

The interim report of the HWG did not recommend the Holocaust – or the Second World War – as topics for study. This decision was reversed and the Holocaust was included, as an aspect of the Second World War, in the Group's final report. But it is a curiosity that a topic that did not specifically feature in the 1989 interim report should subsequently emerge as a non-negotiable topic for study in its own right.

This chapter reveals the reasoning behind the absence of the topic of the Holocaust from the interim report, and why the HWG subsequently changed its position and suggested in its final report that the two world wars and the Holocaust be taught as part of a compulsory programme of study. The chapter then moves on to discuss the aims and objectives behind the inclusion of the topic of the Holocaust in the National Curriculum for History and the debate in the Jewish press over whether the topic of the Holocaust should be taught in school history.

Based on original research, this chapter draws on personal interviews with four members and the HMI observer of the HWG; telephone interviews which were conducted with two members of the group; and correspondence with a further four group members; as well as HWG documentation and documents from the archives at the HET.

The decision not to name the Holocaust

Between 30 May and 2 June 1989 the HWG met together for the ninth time. This meeting took place at Hebden Bridge in Yorkshire. Roberts was unable to attend the first day of this meeting and arrived on the Wednesday morning (31 May). During this meeting, the HWG discussed curriculum content and 20th-century history. Since Roberts was present at this discussion, it must have taken place during the evening of either 31 May or 1 June 1989.[1] The Group had spent most of the afternoon and the early evening debating curriculum content; the aim of this meeting was to draft an interim report for discussion and amendment (NC/HWG (89) 9th).

Impatient with what appeared to be convincing evidence of the narrow presentation of 20th-century history in many schools, and irritated with what seemed to him a woeful underrating of what might be expected from teachers,[2] John Roberts rose to his feet. For a little under an hour he spoke to the rest of the Group about the 'real' history of the 20th century. His audience listened carefully throughout. By around midnight a decision had been made: the Second World War and the Nazis would be omitted from the interim report as a specific study unit.[3] Roberts convinced the group that the topic of the Second World War and Nazi Germany, 'conventionally regarded as constituting all that was interesting in twentieth century history' (correspondence, 14 May 2002), were important, but did not have the same degree of impact as other events.

Roberts was the only academic historian among the group. He had just completed his book, *The Triumph of the West*. R. Phillips noted in *History Teaching, Nationhood and the State* that, 'by their own admission, members of the History Working Group emphasized the importance of Roberts' influence in the early stages of History Working Group's lifetime' (Phillips 1998: 55). Indeed, this was noted by group members during interviews conducted as part of this study. One member explained that the Group saw the high-profile historian as a defence and insurance against any criticism of their proposals (interview, 24 June 2002).

Roberts' understanding of the 20th century is publicly available; in his *The Penguin History of the Twentieth Century* Roberts argues the Holocaust changed the demography of eastern Europe and had a catalyst effect on the appearance of Israel. As such, the Holocaust is an important topic of study to explain the Middle East situation, the actions of the Muslim world and the suffering of the Palestinian people. According to group members, Roberts' argument was intellectually powerful. He understood the significance of the Holocaust historically, but his long view of history meant that he felt real concern about the representation of the 20th century in schools. Roberts set out his views regarding the omission of the Second World War and the Nazis as named topics from the interim report in a letter he wrote to Supple on 12 October 1989. Despite having resigned from the HWG after the publication of the interim report,[4] Roberts received a number of 'angry and argued letters about the uniqueness of the Holocaust' (correspondence, 14 May 2002). One of these came from Supple; Roberts replied to her letter at some length. This letter set out in detail his argument against a specific programme of study for the Second World War and the Nazis and is summarized here:

The major themes of the last century were the emergence of the USA and Russia as world powers, the development of Asia and the revolution in expectations accompanying unprecedented population growth.

Hitler's personal contribution was to detonate the second phase in the European civil war. His achievements were important but negative and do not compare to the achievements of Stalin who rebuilt the Russian empire of the tsars, a Japan which gave a death blow to European imperialism, and a USA which provided a shelter behind which Europe was rebuilt after 1945.

The Holocaust was a negative result of Nazism. It wiped out centuries-old Jewish communities and changed the sociology of much of eastern Europe for ever. A consequence was the acceleration of the appearance of Israel. However, this was the end of a long, sad story of centuries of anti-Semitism, it did not start in 1939. It was the worst, most savage and brutal collective story of the war, and it was an appalling shock to European sensitivities because no one would have believed it possible in say, 1914. There is, therefore, a repellent but interesting episode in Europe's history to be explored. But the Holocaust did not change history or have the same impact of for example, the Chinese Revolution.
(Taken from a letter to Carrie Supple from John Roberts, 12 October 1989)

Roberts also believed that in terms of teaching about the 'modern' world, 1945 was a better year 'zero': 'we are all aware of the arbitrary nature of starting-dates. You have to take something as "given". Oddly, the world in 1945 is simpler to start with than the world of 1939 (which actually needs to be explained by going back to 1918)' (letter to Carrie Supple from John Roberts, 12 October 1989). The Group's Chairperson, Saunders Watson, said that, 'John Roberts advocated standing back and looking through a telescope at the century, he was very knowledgeable about it. He thought we should convey a feeling rather than be too specific' (interview, 11 July 2002).

In essence, Roberts believed that a curriculum for the 21st century should take the long view and incorporate the events and areas of the world that were of such importance that children of secondary age needed an introduction to them. Such a perspective on history would place the Holocaust among several mass atrocities of the 20th century. At a later meeting following the publication of the interim report, one group member summed up the spirit of Hebden Bridge,

the criteria at Hebden Bridge went beyond present day civics and towards preparing students for the twenty first century. History study units

[HSUs] had been chosen on the basis of relevance to this point – hence one reason for not including Nazi Germany; it was relevant to the present day but not necessary for the twenty first century.
(NC/HWG (89) 14th)

A combination of further arguments prevailed in addition to Roberts's thesis that the Second World War and the Nazis had comparatively less influence on history than did other events. Interestingly, Hobhouse, the only member of the Group to have fought in the Second World War, considered this event (like the only history teacher who recalled the war) too complicated for the classroom. Hobhouse had joined the navy in 1942. In his view, history was not equipped to teach about this period adequately without access to the Russian archives (interview, 30 May 2002). Jones also felt that the Second World War and the Nazis should be omitted. He had two concerns: the first was a question of balance and the second was the level of maturity of the students involved. He explained:

The first of my worries was that the study of the Second World War, which tended to be part of the wider topic of Nazi Germany and obviously included the Holocaust, occupied too central a role in secondary school history. The study of fascism, along with Stalin, in my view, loomed too large in what was now christened Key Stage 3, and was the major subject of study for GCSE. Many pupils then went on to study it for A level as well, and I thought then and I believe even more strongly now, that this concentration on the 20th-century dictatorships was bad for pupils' historical understanding. So this was a question of balance. My second, more fundamental, worry was that the full evil of the Nazi regime, and the Holocaust in particular, could be and perhaps has to be superficially dealt with if it is tackled with pupils below a certain age. These are momentous issues and they do have the fascination of evil. But the newsreels and other images of Nazi Germany which in one way make it eminently teachable, in another way, particularly in the case of the Holocaust, make it too frightening to go into the full story in all its horror. But if you don't go into it in all its horror this is an insult to those who suffered. So, I think that to study these topics requires a substantial historical background and a considerable degree of moral and emotional maturity. My own view was that Nazi Germany and the Holocaust were best studied post-16.
(Interview, 14 May 2002)

Indeed, Roberts had suspected:

> Fascism is studied by a lot of people because of a sort of fascination with it. And I suspect that a lot of the fascination with Nazism is unhealthy. Too much fascination with it arises among the young because it seems glamorous (the cult of uniforms and will) and violent. That's why the media go on about it – it is photogenic in every sense. But what is its real importance? What did it *change*? Nothing like what communism changed by what it did to deflect and isolate Russia.
>
> (Letter to Carrie Supple from John Roberts, 12 October 1989, emphasis in the original)

The History Working Group reconsider

Roger Hennessey was not persuaded, however. Feeling that it was a mistake to omit the two world wars from the interim report, he went to discuss this decision with Saunders Watson the morning after the decision had been made.[5] Hennessey recalls that he predicted an outcry over the omission on publication of the report, and also that he felt concern that there would be a gap in the curriculum if these events were left out and the Russian Revolution included; students would examine the rule of Stalin but not Hitler. He was concerned, he said, about 'the most violent and destructive war in history being omitted from the National Curriculum' (Interview, 20 June 2002). Hennessey thought that the Holocaust could also be approached in terms of events such as the Armenian massacres and the atomic bomb under a heading of 'Major Failures of the 20th Century' (interview, 20 June 2002). However, as far as Saunders Watson was concerned, the decision on whether to include the Holocaust lay with the whole group.

Some group members began to doubt that the right decision had been made shortly after the Hebden Bridge meeting. On 12 June, one group member prepared a paper discussing 'content overload in Key Stage 4' in which she noted:

> I am also concerned about the omission of Nazi Germany and its impact on Europe. It will be an omission which is very hard to explain even though, arguably its 'impact' as an agent for change in the modern world has not been great. It is an area which captures the imagination and interest, not only for reasons of sensationalism.
>
> (Content 'Overload' in Key Stage 4, 12 June 1989)

Several members interviewed felt that there was an element of 'kite-flying' among the Group; reaction to the interim report would be gauged and taken into account when devising the final report. The first draft of the interim report was produced at Hebden Bridge. The Group next met in London between 7 and 10 June where they went through the draft report. The Group was required to give one exemplar programme of study for Key Stage 4; they chose to outline 'Britain in the Twentieth Century'. This exemplar made no reference to the events of the Second World War (DES 1989: 68). The interim report was published on 10 August; the predicted outcry duly came: 'The new curriculum even writes the Nazis out of history with no mention on the compulsory list of the rise and fall of the Third Reich or the First World War' (*Today*, 11 August 1989). However, and significantly, Robert Guyver felt the public's criticism was not based on historical objectives:

> There were many complaints about omissions. The omission of the Second World War was regarded as a foolish error not so much on historical grounds as for moral and ethical reasons. The omission of the First World War met with many complaints.
> (Guyver 1990: 105)

The HWG minutes reveal that a number of responses concerning the teaching of 20th-century events were received following the publication of the Interim Report. During the Group's 14th meeting, an interim report from the responses panel[6] was given in which it was noted a number of responses had been received commenting upon the fact 'that World War Two and the Nazis, the Reformation, and "Medicine Through Time" had been omitted' (NC/HWG (89) 14th). 'Medicine Through Time' was a popular component of the Schools History Project.

During the same meeting, the programmes of study panel suggested modifications to the HSUs. In Key Stage 4, the Group decided to add a new HSU 'The Second World War, its Advent, Course and Aftermath, 1933–1948'. There had been a colloquy of historians held on 5 September at Chatham House in London. A member of the Programmes of Study Panel (who attended the colloquy) first proposed this new study unit to the other members of the panel on 9 September. Two members of the panel in particular worked on this programme of study throughout September. One worked especially hard to inject as much of a world perspective as possible into the unit. The decision to include the Second World War and the Holocaust was accepted by the HWG on 29 September 1989.

Meanwhile, responses regarding the omission of the period of the Second World War continued to be sent to the History Working Group. During the

15th meeting, which took place between 9 and 11 October, responses to the interim report were discussed. Key Stage 4 was the most heavily criticized key stage. One major criticism was that there was too much 20th-century history, but at the same time it was noted that, 'the omission of Fascism, Nazism and both World Wars was the most repeated criticism' (NC/HWG (89) 15th). During the Group's 16th meeting on 20 October the responses panel gave a report during which the most commonly mentioned omissions were stated. The first three on this list of six topics were the Holocaust, the rise of fascism and the rise of Nazi Germany, and the First and Second World Wars.[7]

It is interesting that responses to the interim report cited the Holocaust as a topic in its own right. As noted, the HWG viewed the Holocaust as part of the Nazi period and never discussed it as a topic in its own right, separate from the Second World War.

The Holocaust as history or citizenship?

It was also noted by the responses panel that both the British Legion and Western Front Association wrote about the omission of the two world wars (NC/HWG (89) 16th Annex A), and that 'secondary teachers' perceptions of omissions coincided generally with the perceptions of the wider public response (e.g., WWI/WWII, more European history, etc.)' (NC/HWG (89) 16th). Public reaction to the apparent omission of the Second World War and the Holocaust had an effect on the HWG's original decision, which was reversed despite their misgivings about its inclusion as a compulsory study unit. In a letter, Peter Marshall recalled that when he joined the Group:

> The issue was what sort of modern European history was to be taught and at what stage. The Provisional Report recommended a post-Second World War unit at Key Stage 4. In the abstract, I am sure this had a lot to be said for it, although that decision was taken before my time. Concentrating on the Second World War builds in stereotypes about Britain and its relations with Europe that have little relevance to the world in which young people now live. The recent German Ambassador in London used eloquently to express the reservations that many of us feel on the dead hand that certain views of the Second World War lays on our consciousness of Europe. It turned out, in my view, however, to be an impractical decision that went against, as far as we could judge, the wishes of most teachers as well as arousing the strong opposition of ex-service groups

and those with a concern that the Holocaust should be taught. The latter point was certainly a consideration but not, as I remember it, the decisive one. My sense, and I suspect that of others on the Group, was that we had no alternative to going on with World War Two a bit longer, while hoping that a consensus among teachers would form round a new approach to modern Europe in due time.
(Correspondence, 22 August 2002)

On receiving her reply from Roberts, Supple wrote to other members of the HWG asking for their views on her letter from Roberts. One member of the Group replied to Supple:

> The inclusion of the period 1933–45 in the core in the final report was an acceptance that the needs of future citizens must be take [sic] into account, but could not solely be based on the long world view of the academic historian ... To describe the Holocaust as 'the end of a long sad story' is not a reason for not studying it, and the story of *racism* has *not* ended ... What also seems to me clear is that the approach adopted by the course you put on, which makes history teachers partners in the study of the Holocaust, with teachers of other curriculum areas, is the right one and goes far to meet the objections based on 'historical significance' alone.
> (Letter to Carrie Supple from a member of the HWG, 21 June 1990, emphasis in the original)

What is interesting about these comments is that they indicate that the Holocaust was an important topic for study, but not on the basis of historical criteria but rather because of the topic's role in anti-racist and citizenship education. Marshall notes in the quotation above that it was hoped that history teachers would, over time, reconsider their approach to teaching modern Europe, and Guyver is quoted above, 'the omission of the Second World War was regarded as a foolish error not so much on historical grounds as for moral and ethical reasons' (Guyver 1990: 105). The above quotation from a member of the HWG to Supple indicates that unlike the rest of the National Curriculum for History, the period of the Second World War and the Holocaust were included not on historical grounds, but for broader educational goals. Indeed, the Holocaust was included in the final report as an aspect of the Second World War to be taught from a religious and social perspective.

This is important. If the Holocaust was included in the National Curriculum for History primarily for social and moral reasons, then history teachers teaching from this perspective are doing what was originally expected. But is this the role of school history, and should students not have the opportunity to learn about the Holocaust in a historical context? Marie's practice, discussed in Chapter 1, is an extreme example, but her students were unaffected by the emotional approach she took to her teaching on this topic, because they were unaware of the history of the Holocaust.

Did political pressure influence the HWG's decision?

On 17 April 1989 a member of the HWG, who would later serve on the responses panel, had faxed a list of topics for consideration to the Group's Secretary. Communism and fascism; the rise and fall and rise of modern Germany; the First World War and the Second World War feature in a list of 56 non-British history options. The limited amount of time available for non-British history options may have been a further consideration in the Group's decision to leave the period of the Second World War unnamed in the interim report. Following the publication of the interim report, in an attempt to address the concerns of the Secretary of State for Education and increase the percentage of British history topics in the National Curriculum, the HWG discussed the possibility of listing the Second World War as a British history, rather than a world or European history, unit. A leading member of the Group said that 'if it was considered to be a theme which linked Britain to a world experience, then it would have the same role as the "Reformation" at Key Stage 3' (Minute 6.4, NC/HWG (89) 15th). One member of the HWG said that, 'in fact the amount of British history did not increase in the Final Report; it was cosmetic. As originally written the study unit on the Second World War was widely conceived, as Britain's role was present but not excessive' (interview, 24 June 2002).

However, a cross-party group of MPs considered the Second World War and the rise and fall of the Nazis not to be presentationally British, but an essential part of Britain's glorious past. On the same day the HWG decided to include the study unit 'The Second World War, its advent, course and aftermath, 1933–1948' in their final report, a group of MPs wrote to the Secretary of State for Education and the History Working Group with a 'Submission on the Teaching of the Second World War and the Rise and Fall of Nazi Germany in the National Curriculum for History'. It was signed by Greville Janner, John Marshall, Robert Rhodes James[8] and Jeff Rooker.[9]

The MPs' submission set out the reasons for demanding a place on the History Curriculum for the Second World War and the Nazis:

The decision of the working group to omit any recommendations for the study of these subjects is all the more surprising given the well-known fascination of British people, let alone schoolchildren, for the subject of the Second World War. We remember the war as a series of cataclysmic events; as the first truly 'modern' war; as a fight against fascism and totalitarian dictatorship – and as a conflict in which Britain played a decisive role.

Even today – 45 years after the cessation of hostilities – its legacy affects hundreds of thousands of families throughout the country. Surviving relatives daily remember those who gave their lives. Freedom and democracy exist today in large part, thanks to the sacrifice of those who died in the Second World War.
(Submission on the Teaching of the Second World War and the Rise and Fall of Nazi Germany in the National Curriculum for History)

The MPs concluded their submission:

We regard the omission of the Second World War and the rise and fall of Nazi Germany from the National Curriculum as totally unacceptable; without logic; educationally unsupportable; and offensive to all those who fought in or suffered from the Nazis or the Second World War. It is also a sad signal for the future, if our educational curriculum chooses deliberately to ignore key aspects of Britain's recent past.
(Submission on the Teaching of the Second World War and the Rise and Fall of Nazi Germany in the National Curriculum for History)

The covering letter argued that the 'overwhelming' press and public interest in the 50th anniversary of the outbreak of the Second World War was a clear indication of the need to put the subject on the History Curriculum.[10]

In reply to the MPs' submission of 29 September, MacGregor wrote that the omission was 'apparent' rather than real. Prochaska noted that the HWG had been concerned to be as unprescriptive as possible. There was in fact no intention to exclude the Second World War and the Holocaust, but the intention was not to include this history on a list of mandatory topics (correspondence, 12 July 2002). In the journal article detailing her experiences on the HWG Prochaska wrote:

Among other difficult choices was the question of World War Two. Although intended in our interim report to be covered from the British perspective in a unit on Modern Britain, it was not given separate space of its own. This much criticized omission illustrates the severe problems

of space, especially at Key Stage 4 ages 14 to 16, where only five terms of history will be studied before the final exams. After a protracted debate before the Interim Report, the Group decided that a curriculum for the twenty-first century did not absolutely require the inclusion of the rise and fall of Nazi Germany, as a period singled out for unique significance from a century of wars, world powers and rivalries etc. There was an opportunity for schools to choose to study the subject as a school designed theme at Key Stage 3, but the fact that it had not been specially singled out caused consternation when the interim report appeared. This big omission was contrasted especially bitterly (and for this we have our own presentation to blame entirely) with the fact that we named History study units on Sport and Society, and Entertainment and Society, though these were never intended to be in any sense compared with the history of World War Two.
(Prochaska 1990: 87–8)

Indeed, there was also scope to include the period of the Nazis and the Second World War as a 'school-designed theme' (SDT). SDTs were intended to provide flexibility for teachers to plan and teach study units of their own choosing. However, the cross-party group of MPs concerned with the teaching of this period rejected this suggestion in their submission:

> Theoretically, this might seem to offer schools (and pupils) the opportunity for adequate study of the 'missing' subjects of the Second World War and the Nazi Holocaust in their History Curriculum.
>
> However, the proposal ignores the effect upon the public examination system of the introduction of the National History Curriculum. The examination system by its very nature has to be geared to what is taught in schools.
> (Submission on the teaching of the Second World War and the Rise and Fall of Nazi Germany in the National Curriculum for History)

If schools decided to teach this topic, there was limited time available for teaching SDTs, and at Key Stage 4 there was no provision for the teaching of a SDT. The Secretary of State wrote to Janner, Marshall, Rhodes James and Rooker suggesting that the Second World War and the Nazis would need to be included in the detailed programmes of study for the Key Stage 4 study unit 'East Meets West' which 'includes post-1945 Europe and could not be studied without reference to Nazi Germany and the Second World War' (letter to Greville Janner from John MacGregor, 11 October 1989). There was also room for the inclusion of this period in the study unit

'Japan: Shogunate to the Present Day'. MacGregor noted that the interim report was a discussion document setting out the provisional thinking of the HWG who were currently drafting the detailed programmes of study to support each of the study units, and that he would send a copy of this correspondence to the Group's Secretary.

The History Working Group was meeting at Great Yarmouth when Education Minister Angela Rumbold told the House of Commons during a parliamentary exchange that the Second World War and Nazism would be in the final report:

> *Mr John Marshall:* To ask the Secretary of State for Education and Science if he will make a statement about the teaching of history within the National Curriculum.
>
> *Mrs Rumbold:* My right hon. Friend and my right hon. Friend the Secretary of State for Wales are waiting for the final report of the national curriculum history working group, which they expect to receive by the end of the year. They will then publish their proposals for the History Curriculum.
>
> *Mr Marshall:* Is my hon. Friend aware that the Interim Report of the working group was greeted with shock and dismay by the many who believe that the causes and history of the Second World War should be part of the national curriculum? After all, 1940 was our finest hour; why is it too fine for the history mandarins?
>
> *Mrs Rumbold:* I can assure my hon. Friend that the proposals of the interim working group have been looked at again by the History Working Group, and that the final proposals will contain full programmes of study on all the units, so that matters can be taken fully into account.
>
> *Mr Janner:* Will the Minister explain her previous answer? Does this mean that the national curriculum will contain the rise and fall of Nazism and the Second World War?
>
> *Mrs Rumbold:* As I understand it, yes.
> (Hansard, H. of C., Vol. 160, Cols 171–172, 14 November 1989)

The Chairperson was surprised and annoyed at this attempt to exert political pressure on the Group. He telephoned the DES and made the point that HWG was independent and would make up its own mind about including or excluding content.[11] One member of the HWG who spoke to R. Phillips about this incident said:

We did resent this apparent attempt to influence what we were doing. In fact, we had already decided to include World War Two partly because we heard through the officials that the Government wanted it to be included and partly because it was left out of the original Interim Report on the basis of a very slight majority.
(Phillips 1998: 80)

According to Phillips, 'the significance of the statement was clear; this was apparently a direct attempt by the Government to dictate what historical content should be included in the Final Report' (Phillips 1998: 79). However, as noted, individual members had doubts about the decision to exclude this period as a programme of study from the interim report almost as soon as this decision had been made. The decision to include Nazism and the Second World War in the final report had been made by 14 November: this had been agreed by the HWG on 29 September, and Rumbold probably knew this through the civil servants who 'observed' the Group and reported to their superiors on the discussions that took place; this information would in turn pass up the chain. Rumbold herself appears to endorse this explanation in her statement to Janner: 'as I understand it [from the "observers" keeping the Education Department informed] yes [these subjects feature in the final report]'. This parliamentary exchange is more revealing in terms of politicians' interpretation of the Second World War and the Holocaust, which is discussed below, than the Government's role in exerting political influence and shaping educational policy.

The discourse of John Marshall and Janner was thoroughly different from that of Roberts who had wanted students to be encouraged to take a longer and wider view of history. Roberts was not advocating ignoring the recent past or arguing that this period was unimportant, but as an historian was perhaps able to detach himself from the present time in a way others were unable to do. Janner *et al.* argued that the Second World War was important from the perspective that it cast light on the division of Europe. The Berlin Wall came down 43 days after the MPs made their submission. The National Curriculum for History was being constructed at the same time as 50th anniversaries of key events in the Nazi and Second World War period and at the end of the Cold War. The fall of the Berlin Wall marked the end of this era and the beginning of a period in which Europe, and Germany in particular, would begin to try to come to terms with the Nazi past (Niven 2002). The HWG did not operate in a cultural vacuum and in this sense there can be no doubt that the Group was under pressure to produce proposals acceptable to the Government and the public. It could be argued that the media attention and popular consciousness and interest in the Second

World War and the Nazis meant that it was almost impossible for Roberts's call for a longer and wider view to be heard.[12]

The HWG witnessed adverse reaction to their initial proposals in the press, and some members were themselves uneasy with the decision not to name the two world wars and the Holocaust in the interim report. It is perhaps more than a coincidence that the HWG began work on a study unit on the topic of the Second World War and the Nazis directly following the colloquy of historians. However, the Chairperson appeared determined that the work of the Group would be its own. On balance, it would seem that the decision to include the Second World War and the Nazis was made by the Group in light of the reaction to their interim report.

Interpretations of the Second World War

John Marshall's interpretation as revealed in the parliamentary exchange quoted on page 100 is particularly interesting. He views the period of the Second World War as Britain's 'finest hour', presumably referring to the allies' defeat of fascism and the liberation of the concentration camps. However, Wasserstein's *Britain and the Jews of Europe 1939–1945* describes and explains the near total ban on Jewish refugee immigration to Britain during the war; the restrictive immigration policy in Palestine; the internment and deportation of aliens in Britain; the abortive Bermuda conference on refugees in 1943; the failure to aid Jewish resistance in Europe; and the rejection of the scheme for the bombing by the allies of Auschwitz (Wasserstein 1979). Indeed, as noted in the previous chapter, Lawton had suggested in his lecture to teachers in 1985 that 'the indifference to a considerable extent of the allies deserves some mention. It's not all we're good, they're bad' (ILEA 1985).

Further, it would appear that John Marshall and Janner have different foci. While Marshall is concerned to see the Second World War included in the history curriculum, Janner's focus is the Nazi Holocaust: he broadens the subject of study in the above exchange, asking Rumbold whether Nazism will be taught. On 27 March and 2 April Janner asked in the House of Commons when the final report would be available (Hansard, H. of C., Vol. 170, Col 173, 27 March 1990; Hansard, H. of C., Vol. 170, Col 421, 2 April 1990).[13] During the exchange with Rumbold on 14 November 1989, Janner's concern had been over whether Nazism would be included in the final report. However, on 4 April he asked the Secretary of State for Education what steps he intended to take to introduce the study of the Nazi Holocaust into state schools as a *core part* of the National Curriculum (Hansard, H. of C., Vol. 170. Col 621, 4 April 1990).

Should the Holocaust be taught in school history?

Fox was also clear in his commitment to Holocaust education. He had helped the cross-party group of MPs to prepare their submission and defended their position in an article in the *Jewish Chronicle* on 12 January 1990 following the publication of a piece by Lionel Kochan, which appeared in the newspaper on 22 December 1989, arguing against the teaching of the Holocaust. Kochan began his piece:

> In the past few weeks, the Secretary of State for Education received a letter from the president of the Board of Deputies [Janner] and a group of sympathetic MPs, protesting at the proposed exclusion of the post-1939 period for the new history syllabus for schools. He also received a letter from me, welcoming this exclusion.

His argument was that 'disseminating a knowledge of Nazi barbarism was fraught with danger and that the Holocaust, whether taught at school or at university, was best omitted from the syllabus'. David Sorkin wrote to the *Jewish Chronicle* in support of Kochan's view, 'if we choose to focus on the Holocaust, we select that aspect of Jewish history which, to be sure, unfailingly appeals to the emotional voyeur, but in the end we sell the Jews and Judaism short, as well as giving the discipline of Judaic studies a bad name' (*Jewish Chronicle*, 9 February 1990). Teaching the Holocaust would not prevent a repetition of this event, said Kochan; furthermore, he asked, 'Who would be a Jew if suffering and persecution were the dominating themes of our history?' and 'Why should massacre and bloodshed be the dominating themes presented to schoolchildren and students?' However, Fox responded:

> Ignorance and incomprehension about the significance of Holocaust education and research I expected – and received – in response to the questionnaires I sent out for the survey on teaching the Holocaust which I conducted on behalf of the Yad Vashem academic and educational subcommittee. I did not expect it from the likes of Lionel Kochan.

Fox argued that the Holocaust should not be perceived solely as *Jewish* history but rather as an event which belonged to humanity:

> The subject (in its widest sense) is of concern to all, non-Jew and Jew alike. Not only must one examine its contemporary significance, one must also consider its historiographical importance. It is imperative, therefore, that it takes its rightful place in the school and university curriculum.

Fox stressed the importance of teaching the Holocaust in order to protect the historical and moral memory of this phase in history, questioning whether Kochan was 'serious that this seminal segment of modern Jewish history should be wiped out of educational – and indeed moral – memory?' However, Kochan did not believe the subject of the Holocaust should not be studied, but rather that it was inappropriate for study by undergraduates:

> I do not argue that the Holocaust should not be *studied*. I do not subscribe to the view of those who see it as a mystery, as something so far removed from the normal experience of humanity as to have taken place in another world entirely, and thus incomprehensible. On the contrary, here is the work of human beings, and what certain human beings have done other human beings can try to make explicable. But there is a world of difference between scholarly research and teaching to the immature and unsophisticated.

Kochan highlights one of the difficulties of teaching the Holocaust: teachers need to be aware that they may inadvertently put over the view that the Jews are victims or did something to deserve their treatment. This was Kochan's primary concern: 'those who "teach the Holocaust" are, in fact, doing the future of Jewry the greatest possible disservice. They are teaching a whole generation to regard us in a particularly vulnerable light' (Fox, 12 January 1990; Kochan, 22 December 1989).

On 28 November 1990, the Institute of Contemporary History and Wiener Library held a debate 'Teaching the Holocaust: For or Against?' between Kochan with Sorkin and Ronnie Landau with Philip Rubenstein. The *Jewish Chronicle* reported that some Holocaust survivors made 'angry comments' following Kochan's speech (7 December 1989). Several points should be noted about the intense level of debate amongst the Jewish community and scholars of Jewish history regarding the teaching of the Holocaust in school history and what this indicates: first, this is another reminder that at the time the National Curriculum was being constructed, the Second World War was in living memory. The issue of historical objectivity and 'detachment' (Evans 1997: 252) is relevant here. It was unlikely that many people would be able to take a long view and construct a history curriculum for the 21st century with the necessary detachment. Second, this level of debate was a clear indicator of the need for wider debate and discussion of the question, 'What is the rationale for teaching the Holocaust in history?'

The rationale behind the inclusion of the Holocaust in the History Curriculum

The construction of the National Curriculum presented an opportunity to those who were committed to Holocaust education to ensure that the Holocaust be taught in schools as part of the mainstream syllabus. The absence of the Second World War and the Nazi Holocaust from the interim report was of concern to those who had throughout the 1980s been working to establish the teaching of the Holocaust in schools. Landau wrote to the *Jewish Chronicle*, 'it is scandalous that serious study of the Nazi regime and the Holocaust may be consigned to oblivion. For under the proposed scheme, hardly anyone below the age of 16 would ever study it in school – a truly alarming turning back of the clock' (*Jewish Chronicle*, 25 August 1989). The introduction of the National Curriculum meant that if the topics of the Second World War and the Holocaust were included teachers would apparently *have* to teach about them.

Mindful of my own classroom experience and of the pedagogical concerns raised by Kochan outlined above, I asked Fox in an interview in January 2004 how he envisaged or wanted the Holocaust to be dealt with in school history:

I have absolutely no idea is the short answer with regard to the school level. So far as universities were concerned it was much easier because what I wanted at university level was for it to be taught as a special subject to be included as part of a general history degree course and an important element of any special subject on Nazi Germany, but my ideal aim, this is what I always wanted to do, was teach a special subject on 'the Holocaust' at university. As far as schools I had no real idea, I must admit. It was generally to promote greater awareness of it. By then I was way out of school. I taught in schools for seven years from 1962 to 1969.
(Interview, 21 January 2004)

Once the place of the Holocaust had been secured on the History Curriculum, the Chairperson of the HET turned his attention to ensuring that teachers had the necessary support to teach the Holocaust, and to that end argued *cross-curricular* short-courses be provided:

It is vital that Holocaust education in Britain includes the concepts and issues which have been developed in Jewish Holocaust education over the last 45 years and which have proved so essential.

We believe that the organization of a series of Holocaust at Key Stage 3 cross-curricular short courses for LEA advisers, teachers and Heads of Department, might best serve its teaching.

(Letter to Ken Oldfield from Greville Janner and Merlyn Rees, 12 November 1991)

History teachers' objectives may well have been blurred by the cross-curricular nature of the topic of the Holocaust, which even the member of the HWG who wrote to Supple saw as being more important in terms of anti-racist education than in terms of historical significance. But perhaps more significant than this blurring of the role of the Holocaust in the National Curriculum for History is the issue that apparently no consideration was given by those who campaigned for the inclusion of this topic in the National Curriculum of, as Plowright wrote in reaction to the Fox Report, 'first principles such as establishing the importance of teaching the Holocaust and teaching it in a particular manner' (1991: 26). Rather, campaigners such as Fox concentrated on winning the argument and securing the inclusion of the period of the Second World War and the Holocaust in the National Curriculum for History. As the following chapter discusses, there has been no debate or agreement to date at a curriculum decision-making level regarding 'first principles' and the teaching of the Holocaust in school history.

Chapter 5

Teaching the Holocaust in school history since 1991

The previous chapter has demonstrated that a clear rationale regarding what was important about teaching the Holocaust in school history was lacking among those who shaped the original National Curriculum for History. It was social and moral reasoning, more than historical criteria, which resulted in the inclusion of the Holocaust in the HWG's final report.

Drawing on interviews with individuals who took part in the two reviews of the National Curriculum for History that have since taken place, and correspondence with the Qualifications and Curriculum Authority (QCA), this chapter reveals that while the topic of the Holocaust has gained increasing prominence in the school history curriculum, there has been no opportunity to discuss and theorize the teaching of the Holocaust in school history, or the purpose of school history more generally.

The Dearing Review

Thatcher concludes her writing on the National Curriculum in her memoirs commenting that by the time she left office in November 1990 she 'was convinced that there would have to be a new drive to simplify the National Curriculum and testing' (Thatcher 1993: 597). Thatcher's understanding of the National Curriculum was different from that envisaged by Baker, and from the final form that it took. In an interview for the *Sunday Telegraph* in April 1990, Thatcher explained her understanding of the core curriculum, going on to point out, before it had been completed, where it had gone wrong:

> The core curriculum, so far as we have got the English one out, the mathematics and the science – now that originally was what I meant by a core curriculum. Everyone simply must be trained in mathematics up to a certain standard. You must be trained in a language and I would say some literature up to a certain standard, you really must. It is your own tongue. It is not enough to be able to speak it: you must know some of

the literature. And you simply must have the basic structure of science. And you must not be allowed to give them up before you are 16 ... When we first started on this, I do not think I ever thought they would do the syllabus in such detail as they are doing now. Because I believe there are thousands of teachers who are teaching extremely well. And I always felt that when we had done the core curriculum, the core syllabus, there must always be scope for each teacher to use her own methods, her own experience, the things which she has learned and she or he knows how to teach.

(*The Sunday Telegraph*, 15 April 1990)

Baker, on the other hand, believed that a radical overhaul of the curriculum was required, and that this could only be achieved through strong centralization and the establishment of a broad entitlement curriculum (Baker 1993). Given the lack of a single vision and consensus over the National Curriculum, it is unsurprising that its original form was rapidly revised.

Margaret Thatcher resigned as Prime Minister in November 1990; she was succeeded as Leader of the Conservative Party and Prime Minister by John Major, who went on to win the 1992 General Election. It became clear to John Major's Government that the National Curriculum framework and related testing arrangements could not survive in their original form. Concerns that the tests involved excessive workload and were educationally unsound led the three largest teaching unions, the National Union of Teachers (NUT), the National Association of Schoolmasters/Union of Women Teachers (NASUWT) and the Association of Teachers and Lecturers (ATL) to ballot members on a boycott of all National Curriculum tests (Chitty 2002: 72). John Patten, who had replaced Clarke as Secretary of State for Education in April 1992, was finding it difficult to command respect from parents and teachers alike. In April 1993 he announced that a review of the National Curriculum would be conducted by Sir Ron Dearing. Dearing was the Chairperson-designate of the new School Curriculum and Assessment Authority (SCAA) to be established in October 1993.

The Dearing Review was politically important and had to be successful. Teachers had to feel that the curriculum had been revised and provided a workable framework, and these revisions would have to be acceptable to the general public – parents and voters. Dearing's interim report, *The National Curriculum and its Assessment* was published on 2 August 1993. Complaints regarding curriculum overload and the level of prescription were accepted and an explanation as to why the original National Curriculum had in the process of its development come to take such a form was put forward. In part, this explanation supports Lawton and Chitty's conviction that the National Curriculum was fundamentally flawed due to the fact it was conceived of entirely in terms of subjects (Lawton and Chitty 1988):

> The problem of curriculum overload stems, in part, from the fact that original Working Groups established to define the content of each Order were not able to judge the collective weight in teaching terms of the Curriculum *as a whole*. Neither was it possible to avoid some overlap of content *between* subjects. A further problem stems from the fact that the attempt to spell out the requirements of each National Curriculum subject in a clear, unambiguous manner has led to a level of prescription that many teachers find unacceptably constricting. The balance between what is defined nationally and what is left to the exercise of professional judgement needs to be reviewed.
> (NCC/SEAC 1993: 50–6)

The interim report was welcomed by the Government. Baroness Blatch, deputizing for Patten, who was ill when the report was published, announced on behalf of the Government, 'we accept the report in its entirety' (quoted in Chitty 2002: 81). Dearing's final report was published on 5 January 1994. With regard to curriculum content, Dearing recommended a reduction in the statutory content of the National Curriculum and that a core of compulsory material should be separated from optional subject matter.

Clarke's intervention at Key Stage 4 to allow students to opt for either history or geography was not only upheld but furthered as Dearing recommended both subjects become optional. Chitty remarks that 'as far as the provision for older students was concerned, it is fair to say that Sir Ron Dearing's Final Report effectively marked the end of the National Curriculum for those beyond the age of 14' (Chitty 2002: 84). Working parties, which were once again carefully selected by government ministers, now began to review all of the National Curriculum subjects. The new arrangements they decided upon would be introduced in September 1995 and teachers were promised no further changes to the National Curriculum for at least five years.

The SCAA Advisory Group for History

The SCAA Advisory Group for History met for three two-day meetings between January and February 1994. The group comprised 14 individuals in total: a primary head teacher, four classroom teachers, an academic with special-needs expertise, an LEA adviser, the Head of Education at the

British Museum, a member of SCAA, an Ofsted HMI inspector, three SCAA representatives and a DfE observer. Group members were selected and invited by SCAA to take part in the review. The Group was apparently constituted in such a way as to attempt to placate all sides in the history debate as far as possible and to minimize criticism of the revised history curriculum in the press.

The SCAA Advisory Group for History was subject to greater political control than the HWG. Whereas Saunders Watson had defended the HWG's right to make decisions independently, one member of this Group told me that the Chairperson of the SCAA Advisory Group for History used language such as, 'I don't think that will be acceptable' or 'I'm sure that would not be acceptable' in response to suggestions from the Group (interview, 28 May 2003). It is significant that the word used was 'acceptable', rather than 'appropriate' for example, as it indicates that the Chairperson was talking about the need to please the Department for Education and SCAA.

There were additional pressures on the SCAA Advisory Group for History, just as there had been on the HWG. This was a high-profile review which received considerable media coverage – so much so that the locations of the meetings of the SCAA Advisory Group for History were kept secret from the press. Chris Woodhead, who at the time was the Chief Executive of the SCAA, was concerned to keep as much adverse publicity out of the press as possible. Nonetheless, headlines such as 'Past a Joke' appeared in *The Sun*, criticizing the proposal from 'a leaked report' that Trafalgar, Waterloo, the Battle of Hastings and the Gunpowder Plot should become optional and questioning 'How can you be proud of your country if you don't know its history?' (*The Sun*, 1 March 1994).

The views of Christopher McGovern, one of the members of the SCAA Advisory Group for History, also made headlines in the *Daily Mail* (15 March 1994) and the *TES* (18 March 1994) after he wrote a five-page letter to Dearing criticizing the Group's work and recommendations. McGovern desired a greater amount of uniquely British history in the curriculum and bewailed the fact that the Great Fire of London, the Gunpowder Plot and the Plague of 1665 were not compulsory. Like the period of the Second World War in the HWG's original proposals (DES 1989), these topics were unnamed but there was scope for teachers to teach about these events if they wished. Professor Anthony O'Hear, who was a member of the SCAA Advisory Group for History, and was described like McGovern as a right-wing historian, rejected McGovern's criticisms. He was quoted in the *Daily Mail*:

It is true that the Plague of 1665 and the Great Fire of London are not specifically mentioned, but this does not mean they cannot be taught. Nor do I think that curriculum is symptomatic of a national crisis. Can it really be pretended that the Plague and the Fire are key political events, on a level with the Civil War, the Interregnum and the Restoration, all of which are mentioned in the Stuart period?
(*Daily Mail*, 15 March 1994)

The notion that if topics were compulsory in the National Curriculum they would be taught, but if they were not named they would not be taught, comes over in the article published in *The Sun* on 1 March 1994: 'Sorry, Nelson. Hard luck, Wellington. You could soon be history. The heritage of Britain should become optional at school says a leaked report. Children wouldn't have to learn about Trafalgar, Waterloo, the Battle of Hastings or the Gunpowder Plot'. This notion that non-compulsory topics would not be taught by teachers (and that compulsory topics would) was shared by some members of SCAA Advisory Group for History. One member was particularly struck by the gulf between the position of politicians and policy-makers and their own experience of the classroom. They saw their role as attempting to get over to other, non-teaching members of the Group, the reality of what actually happens in the classroom. Comments made by teachers in Chapter 1 demonstrate that listing a topic as compulsory does not necessarily mean that it will be taught. As noted, this is not only the case for the Holocaust, but also for the Cold War, which Tom commented he hardly had time to touch upon.

Another issue highlighted by McGovern's criticisms is the difficulty in developing a curriculum upon which there is no consensus; this is demonstrated by the apparent 'split in the traditionalist view' (*TES*, 18 March 1994). The slimming down of the National Curriculum for History was complicated by the fact that the subject was no longer compulsory at Key Stage 4 as had been envisaged by the 1988 ERA and devised by the History Working Group. The SCAA Advisory Group for History was presented with the challenge of both slimming down and expanding national-curriculum content which, as one member of the Group recalled, 'in itself was a major issue' (interview, 28 May 2003).

In the time devoted to discussion of curriculum content[1] 'the twentieth century problem' (interview, 28 May 2003) was deliberated. Deliberations centred upon whether to introduce additional HSUs on the 20th century from Key Stage 4 into Key Stage 3, or to expand the existing Key Stage 3 study unit 'The Era of the Second World War' (which had been moved from Key Stage 4 to Key Stage 3 by Clarke in response to criticism that if students could take either history or geography in Key Stage 4, they would miss out on learning about the 20th century). This was a core study unit which stated:

> Pupils should be taught about the causes, nature and immediate consequences of the Second World War. The focus should be on the developing conflict between democracies and dictatorships in Europe in the 1930s, the impact of the war on soldiers and civilians, and post-war reconstruction.
> (DES 1991: 45)

This presentation of the Second World War was in line with J. Marshall's interpretation of this period. The unit encompassed developments in Europe since the 1930s, the experiences of war and the immediate consequences of war. However, on its own it could not adequately teach students about the experience of the 20th century. The SCAA Advisory Group for History, therefore, decided to expand this study unit and rename it 'The Twentieth-Century World' (DfE 1995: 13). The fact that history was being truncated meant that the Group had two major considerations when deliberating curriculum content: what the ultimate ignorance would be and what students could not leave school without a knowledge of, as well as tacit assumptions regarding what the public would and would not accept. A member of the SCAA Advisory Group for History explained there was an assumption among the Group that the Holocaust would have to be on the revised curriculum and would have to be named (interview, 28 May 2003).

The Holocaust had been named in the 1991 curriculum. But in that more prescriptive version, it was listed as a topic students should be taught about under the experience of war, along with the experience and impact of war in Europe, Asia and other parts of the world; the role of wartime leaders, including Hitler, Churchill, Stalin and Roosevelt; the home front in Britain and the dropping of the atomic bomb. In the 1995 curriculum, teachers were asked to give an overview of the Second World War, including the Holocaust and the dropping of the atomic bombs and the legacy of the Second World War for Britain and the world. The home front in Britain was moved into Key Stage 2 and the role of wartime leaders became exemplary information of one topic which could be taught in depth. In their dual aim of slimming and expanding the curriculum the SCAA Advisory Group for History enhanced the position of the Holocaust in the National Curriculum for History, but did not consider or establish 'first principles' (Plowright 1991).

The History Task Group 1998–9 and the current position of the Holocaust

The new Labour Government swept to power on 1 May 1997. Tony Blair (the new Prime Minister) had espoused a commitment to 'education, education, education' throughout the general-election campaign. The Government announced a review of the National Curriculum which aimed to focus the school curriculum on outcomes, rather than dictating exactly what should be taught. Thus teachers were to be given greater flexibility by cutting down on the compulsory aspects while retaining the breadth and balance of the curriculum which would be more closely matched to the needs of school students. The aim of the 1998–9 review was made clear to members of the Task Group during their first meeting: this was to further streamline the National Curriculum and to remove as much prescription as possible, allowing teachers greater flexibility. It was different from the Dearing Review in that it was much more low key. The History Task Group was put together by the QCA.[2]

The Group included nine teachers: four from primary schools and five from secondary schools, most of whom were heads of history. There was one LEA representative and one representative from higher education, in addition to 'observers' from Ofsted and the DfES and the QCA history subject officers. The Principal Officer for History at the QCA, Gill Watson, chaired the Group's five meetings. The agenda was predetermined and set by the QCA for all subject groups.

James Arthur has written that the teachers on the Group, particularly teachers from Key Stage 3, were initially reluctant to make further changes to the history national curriculum. However, after 'persuasion' from 'observers' there was a realization that many history teachers had perceived the programmes of study more as a syllabus than a curriculum framework. Teachers had also slimmed down the history curriculum, but not always in a consistent way across the programme of study (Arthur 2000: 2–3). One of the Group's tasks was to outline a clearer rationale for history by stating the priorities of each key stage. However, Arthur has written:

> It would be a mistake to think that the History Task Group generated, far less discussed, a series of issues for history teaching. The Group did not have time to deliberate at any length and was focused on the work of reducing the content specification of the History Order and incorporating statements about the rationale for history teaching, including statements on ICT [information and communications technology] and access.

The Group was largely preoccupied with technical points and getting the right phrases for ideas that had been largely formed elsewhere.
(Arthur 2000: 3)

The review was really about showing links to other subjects, indicating opportunities for social, moral and spiritual development and asking questions such as 'How do you make history more inclusive?'

The National Curriculum for History published in 1999 included a rationale, stating the importance of history:

History fires pupils' curiosity about the past in Britain and the wider world. Pupils consider how the past influences the present, what past societies were like, how these societies organized their politics, and what beliefs and cultures influenced people's actions. As they do this, pupils develop a chronological framework for their knowledge of significant events and people. They see the diversity of human experience and understand more about themselves as individuals and members of society. What they learn can influence their decisions about personal choices, attitudes and values. In history, pupils find evidence, weigh it up and reach their own conclusions. To do this they need to be able to research, sift through evidence, and argue for their point of view – skills that are prized in adult life.
(DfEE 1999: 14)

This statement about the importance of history is reminiscent of the list of aims of school history given by the HWG in its interim (DES 1989) and final reports (DES 1990). Again, history is presented as a compromise between the traditional and the 'new' or alternative traditions.

The purpose of school history

Indeed, there are differing views among historians and educationalists regarding the purpose of school history. Slater wrote in *Teaching History in the New Europe*, 'history is an unsettling and sometimes uncomfortable subject. It is controversial and very often sensitive. There is some consensus about its importance but much less agreement about what it is *for*' (Slater 1995: xi, emphasis in the original). Husbands *et al.* begin the first chapter of their book by discussing the hijacking of the four passenger planes on 11 September 2001 – three of which were flown into the World Trade Center and the Pentagon building, the fourth crashing into the

Pennsylvania countryside (Husbands *et al.* 2003: 3–7). The events of 11 September provide a recent example where history teachers have been called upon to help students try and understand the modern world; in the days following 11 September, some students went to their history teachers to talk about what had happened and why (Godsell 2001). History is an important subject for learning about and understanding the world as it is. Indeed, it was recommended at the 1991 Council of Europe Conference in Tuusula[3] that history should be compulsory for all students up to age 16 for this reason. The Conference noted that, 'it is impossible to understand the current situation in the Baltic, in the Soviet Union, in Northern Ireland and Yugoslavia without a grasp of history which should be every pupil's right' (quoted in Slater 1995: 29).

In 2005, the Historical Association published posters promoting the study of history to post-14 students, using images including the TwinTowers, with a quotation from civil and women's rights activist Pearl Buck, 'If you want to understand today, you have to search yesterday.' Roberts suggested that the Holocaust was an important topic of study to explain the Middle East situation, the actions of the Muslim world and the suffering of the Palestinian people. Short (1998) has also suggested that teaching the Holocaust might improve understanding between Muslims and Jews (see below). In light of recent events in the Middle East, it seems a shame that Islamic civilization, which was recommended as a compulsory study unit in the HWG's interim report, did not become a compulsory part of the National Curriculum for History. There was, in fact, a greater level of debate among the HWG surrounding the HSU *Islam and the Arabs: C7th–C15th* than there was surrounding the teaching of the Second World War and the Holocaust.

It is worth digressing here to expand on this issue: several members of the HWG interviewed noted that this was more contentious than the teaching of the Second World War and the Nazis. A leading member of the group told me, 'there was no fall-out over the Second World War; Islam was more of an issue. In the end it was decided to leave it as optional' (interview, 11 July 2002). During the 14th meeting on 29 September 1989, the Responses Panel reported that comments on Key Stage 3 had indicated that Islam was an issue, but only in that it was not clear why this was compulsory and the French Revolution optional (NC/HWG (89) 14th, 5.2). The minutes reveal debate about the teaching of Islam during the 15th meeting which took place between 9 and 11 October. The debate began when one member, who was on the Assessment Panel:

> expressed reservations about the fact that schools would have to choose between HSUs on the 'British Empire' and 'Ireland' while 'Islam' was a

compulsory unit. She said that many teachers knew nothing about Islam and there were not enough resources for it; if it was removed from the curriculum because of this lack of resources it would cause political controversy.

This prompted a reminder from a member of the management group of the rationale for making Islam compulsory, which was the importance of having a contrast with Roman/Christian civilization; both civilizations had an impact on Europe. Another member:

> added that Western Christendom interacted with Islam and both HSUs were now balanced by the inclusion of the Reformation. It would also make it possible to look at current issues in a context well removed from the present day. This would also be the only point in the curriculum where teachers would be required to teach a core which was not Euro-centric.

There were further comments from other members, including 'that there had been no objection to Islam's inclusion in any of the responses'; 'that Islam had been an important method of transmission of Chinese and other Oriental thought and technology to the West'; 'that in terms of resources it might be fruitful to consider cross-curricular liaison between Religious Education and history'. Eventually, the inclusion of Islam was put to the vote. One member was out of the room for the vote (NC/HWG (89) 17th, 2.1), another abstained, the Group member who had voiced their concerns and begun the debate voted against, along with one other member. The rest of the Group voted in favour of the inclusion of Islamic civilization as compulsory. The Group member who had begun the debate then 'asked that it should be recorded in the final report that not all decisions taken on content were unanimous' (NC/HWG (89) 15th, 6.6–6.8). The compromise that made Islamic civilization optional was decided at the 17th meeting on 3 November at Crawley. The majority depended on the support, or at least the neutrality, of the management group. Hennessey would have liked to see Islam included as compulsory but felt that if there was disagreement among the Group over this issue, this would be mirrored in the press and public and professional opinion (interview, 26 June 2002). At Crawley, changes to the structure of Key Stage 3 were proposed. The Chairperson felt that this key stage

> still lacked a logical structure and permitted choice that might lead to some pupils being taught nothing about the USA or Russia. Each of the

options whilst worthy in themselves required different rationales to be understood and it was still difficult to explain why some HSUs were options and not core.
(NC/HWG (89) 17th, 7.4)

The proposed revisions to Key Stage 3 made Islam optional, meeting the doubts of the minority and the management group. The member who had been most concerned about the inclusion of Islam as a compulsory unit explained during an interview that:

> The issue of Islam bothered me no end. There were people who wanted Islam as a compulsory unit, but I thought it was wrong. In Birmingham [for example] there were some schools that were mostly Muslim and should be able to select Islam as a topic of study, but to make it compulsory in schools which had few or no Muslim pupils would have caused outrage. They would have asked, 'Why does everyone have to learn about the Muslims? Why doesn't everyone learn about us?' The Hindus, Catholics and Jews would be outraged. It was political dynamite and would have caused unnecessary trouble. You could equally quite easily say that it was high time schools did half a term on Jewish history. In Britain and Europe, Jews are a smaller group but at least as influential in terms of their cultural contribution. There should be a choice, and this was the compromise eventually reached.
> (Interview, 29 July 2002)

It would seem that this Group member largely missed the point. As the Group had been reminded, the rationale for making Islam compulsory was the importance of having a contrast with Roman/Christian civilization. The rationale behind the inclusion of Islamic civilization was historical, not religious. The requirement for all schools to cover a non-European culture at Key Stage 3 has survived all subsequent amendments to the National Curriculum for History, and resources have been created to support the teaching of Islamic civilization. In a globalized world which has witnessed terrorist attacks linked to continuing problems and unrest in the Arab world, it would seem of benefit for students to learn more about Islam and the Arabs. Although making topics compulsory on the history curriculum does not necessarily mean they will be taught, it is a shame that Islamic civilization did not receive more of a focus. Speaking in 1990 on the BBC 2 programme *Clean Slate Special*, Professor Stuart Hall said that:

> At this point in time I would put my emphasis on saying the British need to know something about European and Asian civilizations, because the

questions of race, the questions of nation-state, emphasize the question of multiculturalism. The question of diversity of peoples, the question of balancing the needs of Europe against the rest of the world, are going to be the political and historical questions that shape the next century. And not to know anything about the past of those questions is to disable, to disempower. This is a question of what the British need to be alive in a multicultural society in the next century.
(*Clean State Special*, 17 October 1990)

Academics such as Roberts and Hall were looking for the kind of curriculum that would serve citizens of the 21st century. But this agenda was not shared by the Conservative Government (whose most likely motivations are discussed in the concluding chapter) as is evidenced in their appointment of only two academics to the HWG.

In addition to understanding how we got to where we are, Haydn, Arthur and Hunt (Haydn *et al.* 1997: 27) have also pointed to the value of school history in helping students to develop a critical edge, particularly useful in the modern age. They ask their readers to consider 20th-century events, the era of the spin doctor, media manipulation and sound-bite politics using the words of Longworth (1981) to support their point:

> It does require some little imagination to realize what the consequences will be of not educating our children to the sort of differences between essential and non-essential information, raw fact, prejudice, half-truth and untruth, so that they know when they are being manipulated, by whom and for what purpose.

Such aims highlight the revolution that has taken place in school history in terms of purpose and method during the 1970s and 1980s since Price (1968) wrote her article.

Indeed, although Kinloch has stated that when teaching the Holocaust we should start and end with what happened and why (Kinloch 1998), Haydn views school history as being slightly different from academic history. He looks at historical periods and events and considers how these can help students and how they might impact on their lives when they have left school. He writes, 'if we cannot do justice to a topic such as the Holocaust, what is the point of inflicting history on young people?' (Haydn 2000: 136).

Slater states that school history has intrinsic and extrinsic aims. He suggests that intrinsic learning objectives for school students could include 'knowing the difference between AD and BC, understanding the concepts of "cause" and "change", understanding that historical statements must be consistent with available evidence' (Slater 1995: 126). When teaching the Holocaust, an aim such as to improve students' ability to recognize and respond appropriately to similar events would be described by Slater as extrinsic because such an aim is not concerned with the discipline of history – it is extrinsic to history, it is about changing society. Kinloch argues that school history should be taught as academic history, solely for intrinsic purposes. However, like Haydn – and the statement on the importance of history in the current National Curriculum ('what they [pupils] learn can influence their decisions about personal choices, attitudes and values') – Slater sees history as an opportunity for teaching about wider social issues *provided* that history is the basis for this and that the distinction between intrinsic and extrinsic aims is made. Slater also notes that the intrinsic and extrinsic aims of history cannot always be separated:

> There are irresistible social and ethical reasons for helping young people to live in liberal democratic societies, or be opposed to sexism or racism, but these are broader *educational* aims; they are not historical. However, historical perspectives and thinking can make a crucial contribution to our understanding of race, discrimination and liberal democracy ... Historical, personal and social aims are enmeshed and not always easily unravelled, but their emphasis is different and the distinctions remain. They are none the worse for that, provided, that is, we recognize and publicly declare these distinctions. Broader and extrinsic educational aims may well help us to select issues which will then be studied with intrinsic historical procedures.
> (Slater 1995: 126)

This is reminiscent of the views of Meagher (1999), McLaughlin (1999), and Illingworth (2000). Slater makes clear a further distinction between the intrinsic aims of history, which can be guaranteed, and the extrinsic aims, which history can only enable. In an interview with a member of the HWG, who now works in citizenship education, he commented, using the example of Anne Frank, 'You can say to 16-year-olds "What would you have done?" and they will tell you the right thing to do would be to help her. But that doesn't stop them from joining the BNP because "The Pakkis down the road have all the best jobs"' (interview, 26 June 2002). One of the extrinsic aims of teaching about Anne Frank may be to encourage students to think about their own actions. But is it appropriate within a history lesson to ask students what they would do in an historical situation? Here I come back to the issue of detachment discussed in the introduction. It is impossible to know what any of us would have done in an historical situation, because we were not in that situation. For the same reason it is impossible to judge individuals who were in those situations. According to Salmons:

> We must ensure that in studying this history our students encounter not only the worst of what mankind is capable of but, in the stories of resistance, resilience, self-sacrifice and rescue, they also see the best of human nature. These stories should be included not as role models to be introduced as some form of 'moral instruction' but because an understanding of how ordinary people responded in these extreme and extraordinary times are a part of the historical record and are essential to an understanding of the Holocaust.
>
> (Salmons, correspondence, 29 September 2005)

The position of the Holocaust in the current National Curriculum

In the history curriculum published in 1999 there are only four named topics that must be taught in Key Stage 3 history. These all feature in the unit 'A World Study after 1900' and are the two world wars, the Holocaust and the Cold War (DfEE 1999: 22). Thus, the topic of the Holocaust emerged from the 1998–9 review as a topic in its own right, rather than an element of the Second World War. According to Haydn, under the draft proposals drawn up by the History Task Group, the Holocaust was the '*only* topic specified by name which will be a compulsory part of the History Curriculum' (Haydn 2000: 135, emphasis in the original). There is an issue in naming some events and not others as it is perhaps implied to history teachers that some historical events are more important than others. In May 2002, I wrote an article for the *TES Teacher* about teaching the Holocaust in history (Russell 2002: 27) aimed at highlighting some of the broader issues in teaching the Holocaust. I received one revealing response from a history teacher expressing astonishment that some secondary schools may be tight for time when it came to teaching 'the *only* History topic specified as compulsory' which, as a consequence, this teacher 'spent a great deal longer' teaching about (correspondence, 16 June 2002).

Although the 1998–9 review included a rationale, it did not go so far as to establish and outline the theory behind the selection of curriculum content which, consequently, means that teachers continue to lack a firm theoretical foundation for their work. With reference to teaching the Holocaust in history, the diversity of teachers' views and practice is, as noted in Chapter 2, less surprising, given the lack of consensus over fundamental principles such as what the term 'Holocaust' encompasses. It struck one of the History Task Group members as extraordinary that, 'no discussion of the Holocaust was had on that committee and we were informed by a civil servant that the Holocaust would be compulsory' (interview, 7 January 2003).

According to this member of the History Task Group, a civil servant from the DfES said that the Secretary of State (then David Blunkett) had decided the Holocaust was to be compulsory (interview, 7 January 2003). A leading member of the Group confirmed that despite the main role of the group being to slim down the amount of prescription in the National Curriculum, there was in fact no question of removing the Holocaust (interview, 23 January 2003). There was no discussion regarding what was important about teaching the Holocaust in history, what the term 'Holocaust' encompassed, or how the Holocaust should be taught in school history. Members of the Group were not pleased that they were not allowed to discuss the Holocaust question and that this decision was imposed on the Group. One member of the Group stated:

> I was shocked; this had nothing to do with education. It was not agreed. It was imposed without any guidelines or discussion. I thought that there were more important things to be taught. The merits of it were never discussed. To be something separate like that in the History Curriculum is quite remarkable. I personally objected to just one area being compulsory.
> (Interview, 7 January 2003)

This raises the questions of who decides the content of the curriculum and who should decide. The issue of political lobbying is relevant here. Pressure groups influence government decisions, and it would seem in this instance that the Secretary of State had been persuaded on this issue in advance of the History Task Group. Those keen to promote Holocaust education continued to do so after the introduction of the National Curriculum and the Dearing Review. In 1995, 50 years following the liberation of the Nazi camps, the *Schindler's List* education pack was launched. The Principal Officer for History at the QCA at the time was invited to attend the launch of this education pack. Produced by Universal Pictures, Amblin Entertainment, CIC Video and Film Education – in conjunction with the HET – the pack was sent to all heads of history in secondary schools in the United Kingdom. This complimentary pack contained a copy of the feature film for use in classrooms, a study video and a study guide. The film was mentioned by several of the teachers interviewed for Chapter 1. As Hector has commented, 'Spielberg's *Schindler's List* is the most frequently found Holocaust video in English schools, not least because of Spielberg's generosity in donating a specially edited version to every school in the United Kingdom' (Hector 2000: 108).

If the decision that the topic of the Holocaust should be compulsory was indeed made by the Secretary of State in advance of the History Task Group, then there is also the question of what he saw as being important about the Holocaust. On 10 November 2000, Blunkett was quoted in the *TES*:

> It is important that our children learn about how and why the Holocaust happened and about the victims of Nazi persecution. We must ensure our children understand the value of diversity and tolerance to help achieve a society free from prejudice and racism in which all members have a sense of belonging.
>
> (David Blunkett, quoted in the *TES*, 10 November 2000)

While Blunkett seems clear in this quotation on why he thinks the Holocaust must be taught, it appears he denied the History Task Group the opportunity to discuss and theorize the teaching of the Holocaust in history. It is also of note that Blunkett's comments indicate that he regards the topic of the Holocaust as a tool for combating racism and prejudice. The question of whether teaching the Holocaust from this perspective is the role of history teachers is raised once again.

Teaching the Holocaust in school history: a lesson in history or citizenship?

The current (1999) version of the National Curriculum for History was accompanied by non-statutory guidance from the QCA in the form of a complete set of schemes of work for Key Stage 3.[4] Unit 19 'How and Why Did the Holocaust Happen?' (QCA 2000) is a scheme of work on the Holocaust designed to precede a scheme on the Second World War.[5] Jerome Freeman, Principal Officer for History at the QCA, explained that:

> The Holocaust was included in the DfES/QCA scheme of work for Key Stage 3 history because it is a statutory part of the programme of study for Key Stage 3 and the aim of the scheme of work was always to show teachers how they could cover all these requirements. It was given its own unit because it was felt that to incorporate the Holocaust into a broader unit on the Second World War would not do justice to such an

important and sensitive subject. In addition, *some teachers had requested guidance on how to teach this subject at Key Stage 3*. I should add that the scheme of work is in no way compulsory and teachers are free to disregard it and use their own schemes. This means that teachers are free to approach the teaching of the Holocaust, including the time they spend on it, in a way they feel is most appropriate for their pupils.
(Correspondence, 7 March 2002, emphasis added)

The QCA advises teachers that Unit 19 takes approximately 8 to 11 hours to teach. Because this is non-statutory guidance, it is not compulsory for teachers to follow this or to teach the Holocaust separately from the Second World War. The QCA unit is itself but one interpretation of the Holocaust and its 'lessons' and of how these should be taught. This guidance on teaching the Holocaust has its focus on the Jewish persecution, although it states that the persecution of all of the victims of National Socialism should be taught as part of this unit. It is expected that by the end of the unit:

Most pupils will: show knowledge of how and why the Holocaust happened including the chronology of the Holocaust and the way the persecution of Jewish people developed over time; describe some of the ideas and attitudes underpinning the Nazi persecution of the Jews and other groups; make critical and thoughtful use of a range of sources of information about the Holocaust, including ICT; select, organize and use relevant information in structured explanations of the Holocaust.
(QCA 2000)

This is a much more historical presentation of the Holocaust than the majority of teachers in Chapter 1 presented to their students. It may be that the introduction of the Citizenship Curriculum in September 2002 impacted upon the teaching of several of the teachers interviewed. This certainly may have contributed to Marie's confused approach:

Last year there was also an emphasis on delivering citizenship in history and so I was thinking 'Where can I get this in?' and that probably swayed my decision [to teach the Holocaust from a 'moral' perspective] a little bit as well.
(Marie)

Barbara also commented, 'I don't see how you can teach the facts without looking at the moral issues – especially with the Government's stress on citizenship, because it is an ideal cross-over subject'.

The issue of the purpose of school history and how this might have been impacted upon by the introduction of citizenship is therefore of relevance.

Citizenship is a compulsory National Curriculum subject for Key Stages 3 and 4. The introduction of citizenship to the school curriculum has been used to support the case for school history. Andrew Wrenn has argued that citizenship can improve the status and time history has on the school curriculum (Wrenn 1999). The view that the introduction of citizenship may be a way of securing and improving the position of school history is echoed by Andrew Granath who wrote in the *TES Teacher* in June 2002:

> Probably the best hope for the subject is to argue the case for its inclusion within the citizenship element of the Key Stage 3 strategy. The QCA views history as the most likely single subject to deliver complex citizenship concepts such as democracy, representation, justice and tolerance. (Granath 2002)

The introduction of citizenship has reinvigorated the debate over whether school history should be taught for intrinsic or extrinsic purposes. Some see citizenship as damaging because it is about values education, and overt positions on values can be used to distort rigorous objective history teaching. Research completed by Husbands *et al.* found that:

> Not all our case study schools were comfortable with the notion of political education, however, or at least not in an explicit form. For some, the political understanding and values which can certainly emerge from a study of history should remain relatively implicit. (Husbands *et al.* 2003:128)

Michael Riley, however, is among those who believe that objective historical rigour is not the final product but, circuitously, it takes teachers and students into values (Byrom and Riley 2003, Riley 2000). Kate Hammond has similarly argued (using the example of the Holocaust) that history teachers can use the moral to clamber into the historical (Hammond 2001). In Edition 104 of *Teaching History*, Hammond discussed pupils' moral and historical reasoning in the same lesson sequence indicating that, as Meagher (Meagher 1999) had argued in Edition 94 and McLaughlin (McLaughlin 1999) in Edition 96, historical criteria cannot be isolated and taught independently of moral development. This approach is endorsed by Counsell who argues in her *History for All* paper in the Historical Association's *Past Forward* report (Counsell 2002c) for the need for motivation to be emotionally engaged but intellectually sustained. This is only subtly different from

Riley's position in that he is more comfortable with references to values being overt. Counsell is more cautious about this lest teachers, in the name of citizenship, lead students into judging whether people in the past were 'good' or 'bad' as part of a history lesson. She writes, 'This seems to me unacceptable, and also unnecessary – the humanizing process by which rigorous historical learning affects values, and affects our human sensibility, is indirect, and none the less powerful for being so' (correspondence, 10 June 2003).

   Education for Citizenship and the Teaching of Democracy in Schools: final report of the Advisory Group on Citizenship identified three components that should inform citizenship education:

1   *Social and moral responsibility*: children learning from the very beginning self-confidence and socially and morally responsible behaviour both in and beyond the classroom, both towards those in authority and towards each other.
2   *Community involvement*: pupils learning about becoming helpfully involved in the life and concerns of their communities, including learning through community involvement and service to the community.
3   *Political literacy*: pupils learning about and how to make themselves effective in public life through knowledge, skills and values.
     (QCA 1998: 40–1)

Although it has been left to schools to decide how to implement citizenship education and 'it is almost impossible for any one subject to cover all that is required in teaching Citizenship Education' (Arthur and Wright 2001: 21), Jerome Freeman, Principal History Officer for the QCA has stated that, 'by building on current good practice history departments should be in a strong position to contribute to Citizenship Education' (Freeman 2002: 28). Indeed, the Advisory Group on Education for Citizenship and the Teaching of Democracy singled out history, along with English and geography, as subjects which provide a distinctive contribution to the promotion of citizenship (Arthur and Wright 2001: 30).

   The introduction of the citizenship curriculum means that history teachers have greater scope to link historical examples to citizenship themes and to issues which are relevant today. But how overt teachers should be in their teaching on values remains an issue for debate. As has been noted, Kinloch's difficulty with history teachers dealing with moral questions is that he does not see that it is their role to create a new society. Kinloch has questioned whether it is the role of teachers to produce 'good' citizens (2001). This is an issue. On 29 April 2004, the *Independent* reported that a teacher who was planning to stand in forthcoming European elections as a candidate for the BNP had been suspended from his post. This incident raises questions about the role of teachers as values educators. Slater's point regarding the intrinsic and extrinsic aims of history is also relevant here, as is Salmons' comment that:

> If awareness of the importance of individual action and inaction causes students to reflect on their own role in society then all well and good, but while it is our responsibility to support them in this reflection, it is not our right to shape the history in order that they arrive at the same conclusions as ourselves. Otherwise, we cease to be teachers and become preachers.
> (Salmons, correspondence, 29 September 2005)

What has been the political imperative since *c.* 1994 that makes the teaching of the Holocaust non-negotiable? The answer to this question is much the same as the answer to the question, 'Why did the HWG revise its position and suggest the Second World War and the Holocaust as a compulsory programme of study in their final report?' A combination of increasing popular awareness and social and moral considerations meant that not naming the Holocaust in the revised history curriculum would be too difficult to explain to the public.

The SCAA Advisory Group for History met together for the first time in January 1994. December 1993 had seen the release in UK cinemas of *Schindler's List*. The release of this film brought the topic of the Holocaust into mainstream popular culture, offering a Hollywood-style narrative dramatization of the Jewish experience. The production and release of Spielberg's film was timely. In the USA the Holocaust Memorial Museum had been opened in April 1993. Events from nearly half a century earlier were being remembered and becoming an increasing part of the popular consciousness. Where the HWG had been constructing a curriculum amid 50th anniversaries of key events in the Second World War, the SCAA Advisory Group for History was being asked to reconsider the history curriculum at a time of increasing popular awareness of the Holocaust. This has to have had an impact on the Group which (as one member commented and is noted above) assumed the Holocaust would have to be on the revised curriculum and would have to be named (interview, 28 May 2003).

As noted above, in the 1998–9 curriculum review, there was no question of removing the Holocaust as a named topic from the National Curriculum for History. But, due to the fact that the History Task Group could not discuss it, neither was there any discussion of 'first principles'. The debate regarding the rationale behind teaching the Holocaust therefore continues.

The continuing debate

In a journal article which appeared in *Educational Review* in November 2003, Short once again presented his case against the views of Kochan as well as Novick[6] and Kinloch (all have questioned the social and moral 'lessons' of the Holocaust) (Short, 2003b). Short emphasizes the importance of com- memoration and explaining what happened under the Third Reich to future generations (Short 2003b: 280), as well as social and moral lessons including improving understanding between Muslims and Jews;[7] combat- ing Holocaust denial, anti-Semitism and racism; demonstrating that individ- uals can make a difference and do not have to be bystanders; prompting students to consider and protect the democracies that they live in; and con- sidering whether war criminals should be prosecuted despite the passage of time making convictions less likely (Short 1998: 12–15). Short quotes from the final report of the Advisory Group for Citizenship in his 2003 paper; indeed he stresses the role of the Holocaust in education for citizenship:

> If students are familiarized with the horrors of the *Einsatzgruppen* and the death camps and are helped to see these horrors as the ultimate expression of racist ideology, some of them – those open to rational persuasion – may become sensitive to, and concerned about, levels of racism they would otherwise have overlooked as trivial. The lesson they learn, in other words, is to treat any manifestation of racism with concern ... Stu- dents familiar with the Holocaust can hardly fail to realize the perils of turning a blind eye to evil. Conversely, when they learn about the exploits of rescuers, they will find it hard not to appreciate the value of assisting those in need.
> (Short 2003b: 285)

Short's position is in direct contrast to that of Kinloch. In his report on Holocaust education for the Council of Europe, Short includes the San- tayana 'cliché' and states what he believes the aim of Holocaust education to be:

> If handled intelligently and with sensitivity, it [the Holocaust] may help *some* students to understand and abhor racism in general and anti-Semitism in particular, but it is unlikely to have this effect on all students ... The aim of Holocaust education, then, is not to eradicate anti-Semitism and every other manifestation of racism ... The function of Holocaust education is rather to inoculate the mass of the people against racist and anti-Semitic propaganda and thereby restrict its

appeal to the lunatic fringe. Hitler may never have come to power, and the Holocaust never have happened, had the majority of German people had any real understanding of the racist core of Nazi ideology and where it was likely to lead.
(Short 1998: 15–16, emphasis in the original)

Kinloch questions whether it is the role of teachers to produce 'good' citizens and doubts that Holocaust education can achieve genocide prevention (2001):

Many teachers are clear that there are good reasons to teach young people about the Shoah. In this they are supported by the British Government, which has been resolute in including its study in successive versions of England's National Curriculum for History. Indeed, initial versions of the revised Orders for History for September 2000 included the Shoah as virtually the only prescribed content. The topic also featured extensively in initial proposals for the introduction of Citizenship in secondary schools . . . however, not everyone is agreed that it is the business of schools to turn out 'good citizens' whatever that may be supposed to mean. Nor is there a consensus that the study of the Shoah is necessarily beneficial.

Kinloch goes on:

It is claimed that the study of the Shoah will itself help to make any repetition of the Nazi genocide less likely . . . What reason, if any, is there to believe this to be true? The authors [of one textbook which makes this claim] themselves cite the examples of 1970s Cambodia (Kampuchea), and Rwanda in 1994, as examples of post-Shoah genocides. That these took place at all suggests that the study of one example of mass-murder does not itself prevent another.
(Kinloch 2001: 9)

Kochan takes a similar viewpoint:

If the Holocaust does have a lesson it is this: not that the knowledge of its horrors will deter any future perpetrator, but that any such perpetrator will learn a precedent has been set; that a threshold has been crossed which will serve as a source of encouragement.
(*Jewish Chronicle*, 22 December 1989: 25)

But Short takes issue with this view; he is firm in his opinion that teaching and learning about genocide will prevent future genocides from occurring:

What also has to be borne in mind is that mandatory Holocaust education is a comparatively recent phenomenon and one restricted to a handful of countries. It can thus be argued, quite plausibly and contrary to the critics, that the genocides which have occurred over the past 50 years are the result of there having been too little teaching of the Holocaust.
(Short 2003: 280)

So, Short emphasizes the importance of moral issues in teaching the Holocaust. Throughout the revisions and slimming down of the National Curriculum, the Holocaust has gained prominence and ceased to be an aspect of the Second World War, emerging as an area of study in its own right. However, what is interesting about the publication of the QCA guidance is that Freeman notes it was prompted in part by history teachers requesting guidance on how to teach this topic – an indication that history teachers generally lack clarity of purpose in their teaching on this topic. This is unsurprising given that the debates surrounding teaching the Holocaust in school history, namely, the questions of what the Holocaust encompasses and what the role of school history is, remain unresolved. None of the Groups established to design or review the National Curriculum for History have ever defined or given specific meaning to the Holocaust as a topic in school history.

Conclusion

Implications for the future

In his 1998 review of Burleigh's *Ethics and Extermination*, Kinloch asserted that history teachers will not teach the Holocaust effectively until their objectives are clarified. As is evidenced by Chapter 1, there is a lack of clarity regarding the objectives of teaching the Holocaust in school history. The majority of history teachers interviewed as part of this study taught the Holocaust not as history, but often as something more like PSHE or citizenship. This study has not resolved the issue of what history teachers' objectives should be; instead it has revealed a lack of clarity regarding the objectives of teaching the Holocaust in school history, not only in the classroom but at curriculum policy level, where it would appear that social and moral considerations rather than historical criteria resulted in the topic's inclusion in the history curriculum. In this sense, many history teachers would seem to be focusing on that which was seen to be important by those who have demanded the inclusion of the Holocaust in school history. However, the same research that was conducted by the BBC which found that 60 per cent of young people had not heard of Auschwitz found that this was also true of 50 per cent of people generally. By learning about the Holocaust, students are likely to be moved to ask social and moral questions about what happened. But if these troubling statistics are to be improved, the history of the Holocaust must surely come first. This book highlights the need for discussion (and some consensus) of the question 'What is the rationale for teaching the Holocaust in school history?' In this concluding chapter, the central themes of the book are reflected upon.

For history teachers, the lack of a clear rationale for teaching the Holocaust in school history is compounded by the lack of consensus regarding the basic assumptions which underpin the teaching of this topic such as, for example, what the term 'Holocaust' encompasses. It has been established in Chapter 2 that the related issues of terminology and uniqueness have been well debated in academia, though on the evidence of Chapter 1 this is not necessarily the case for history teachers. As also discussed in Chapter 2, the desire to attribute unique status to the Holocaust appears to be concerned with ensuring its memory and, to that end, ensuring the position of the Holocaust on the school curriculum. But the view that if the Holocaust is perceived as unique its status in the National Curriculum for History is assured and unquestionable is itself questionable. As was discussed, Brown and Davies believe that the Holocaust must be perceived as unique by teachers in order to ensure it is taught in schools. However, this position is problematic. Chapter 2 reflected on the impossibility of teaching the unique and learning something from this, as Elton has written, 'the unique event is a freak and a frustration; if it is really unique − can never recur in meaning or implication − it lacks every measurable dimension and cannot be assessed' (Elton 1967: 11). It seems impossible to argue that the Holocaust is unique and incomparable and that it should be taught for the purposes of genocide prevention. And Short has warned that:

> If teachers believe the subject to be devoid of useful lessons, they might, quite reasonably, demand that it be given a more restricted role in students' education; after all, space on the curriculum is both highly prized and in short supply.
> (Short 2003b: 277)

Further, arguing the Holocaust is unique and enshrining the topic in the National Curriculum has not meant that all students are taught about the topic, or that those who are are taught about the topic sensitively and in sufficient historical detail, as is evidenced in Chapter 1.

History is a subject where events should be analysed, interpreted and debated. In this sense, there is a question regarding whether the history classroom is an 'appropriate' arena for teaching about the Holocaust. Giles Marshall wrote to *Teaching History* in 1999:

> Hitler and the Holocaust represent the serious limits of our abilities as history teachers to provide any genuine understanding and interrogation of sources in the classroom ... Can I, for instance, present without comment one of the primary sources that David Irving uses when discussing Hitler?
> (Marshall 1999)

There are issues surrounding the teaching of the Holocaust in school history which are so challenging and sensitive that, at times, one almost wonders whether it would be better to follow Leonard's example in Chapter 1 and not approach the topic at all, rather than cover it superficially. But Short has written that the absence of the Holocaust 'from the curriculum may well be seen as offering tacit support to the deniers and spur them on to greater efforts' (Short 1998: 11).

The issue of Holocaust denial is interesting. The QCA consulted various individuals and organizations to help develop their scheme of work on the Holocaust (QCA 2000). The Head of Education at the HET explained in an interview in November 2001 that she was asked to look at a draft of the QCA scheme of work and had been uncomfortable with elements of the draft unit which included work on Holocaust denial: 'the Holocaust is not up for debate. It happened. It is not appropriate to look at David Irving and issues of denial at Key Stage 3' (interview, 21 November 2001). Students learning about the Holocaust – from an historical point of view – are presented in school history with such a wealth of evidence that it becomes impossible for them to deny what happened. Holocaust denial is not included in the QCA scheme of work. If the draft scheme of work produced for the QCA contained reference to Holocaust denial,[1] it was perhaps written from the perspective of what should be done, rather than thinking about the audience it was for. The issue of why some people deny the Holocaust could be discussed with students. Though students in Year 9 may indeed be too young to discuss this as part of their syllabus, why are they denied the right to learn about the Holocaust later in their school careers? The Holocaust is currently taught to students in England four years before they gain the franchise, with the majority never studying history subsequently. Counsell wrote in one editorial in *Teaching History*:

> It's an old story and a true one. Our Year 9 pupil, Melanie, enjoying history enormously but struggling with factual information that is so new to her, is asked to do a little test. Can she remember just one European dictator? Mussolini? Hitler? Stalin? Melanie tries to remember the lively lessons. Her teacher worked hard to build narratives in her head. But it's all too difficult. Mustering her memory, she thinks she's got there. She's remembered. She writes '*Mutlin*'. Armed with her hybrid dictator, Melanie will be forced to give up history in four weeks' time. In four years' time, she will vote.
> (Counsell 2002a)

If students' compulsory study of history ended at 16 rather than 14, as originally envisaged by Baker, the need for the new citizenship curriculum – introduced in September 2002 and compulsory for students in Key Stage 3 and 4 – may be reduced. According to Phillips, 'the current Citizenship Orders in England place too much emphasis upon civic action at the political level and perhaps not enough on social justice' (Phillips 2002: 145).

If one of the main aims of the citizenship curriculum is, as it would seem to be, to engage young people in our democracy, then Counsell is right to question whether the citizenship curriculum represents an undue loss of faith in the National Curriculum (Counsell 2002b).

On the other hand, given that we in the UK now have a citizenship curriculum and – as is noted in Chapter 3 – given that the Holocaust does not sit easily within any one subject boundary, the topic of the Holocaust may make greater sense as part of citizenship education. David Lambert, Chief Executive of the Geography Association, has argued that subject boundaries need to be broken through if school students are not to be denied an understanding of what it is to be human. Lambert argues that citizenship should be at the centre of humanities teachers' work (Lambert 2004). The construction of the National Curriculum apparently presented an opportunity to those who were committed to Holocaust education to ensure that the Holocaust be taught in schools as part of the mainstream syllabus. Of all the subjects a National Curriculum was devised for, the Holocaust fitted best within the curriculum for history. However, Lambert writes that 'the Holocaust, in particular, puts in front of social science's constituent disciplines particularly difficult questions because of the enormity of the event' (Lambert 2004: 42). While 'conventionally, the Holocaust is perceived as history's property' (Lambert 2004: 43), Lambert uses the example of the Holocaust to argue that all subject specialists in the humanities and social sciences should 'think flexibly and boldly about what their disciplines bring to serving students' educational entitlement rather than defending "subjects" in a series of never-ending turf wars' (Lambert 2004: 48). Indeed, Maitles and Cowan have written a paper advocating teaching the Holocaust to pupils in Scotland aged between 9 and 11 (Maitles and Cowan 1999), citing as one of their reasons for arguing this that primary-school teachers are more likely than secondary-school teachers to adopt a cross-curricular, multidisciplinary approach and, thus, are better able to respond to their pupils' concerns immediately and with flexibility.

But for the time being, the Holocaust remains enshrined in the National Curriculum for History at Key Stage 3. In examining the position of the Holocaust in the history curriculum, another key debate has been considered: the purpose of school history. Kinloch's view, encapsulated in his comment that when teaching the Holocaust in history teachers should 'start and end with what happened and why' (Kinloch 1998: 46) is that school history should be taught for intrinsic purposes. Haydn, on the other hand, contends that school history is subtly different from academic history and provides a basis from which wider social lessons can be taught: 'if we cannot do justice to a topic such as the Holocaust, what is the point of inflicting history on young people?' (Haydn 2000: 136). The debate is about the historical versus moral purpose of school history, the 'great tradition' versus the 'alternative' tradition, the polemic argument between Carr (1961) and Elton (1967). Rather than resolving this debate and providing a clear rationale for school history, the National Curriculum for History 'was based around a policy of compromise which appeared to hold the two traditions in creative tension' (Husbands *et al.* 2003: 13). As was noted in Chapter 5, subsequent reviews of the National Curriculum conducted in 1994 and 1999 have done little to clarify the situation. The 1995 curriculum contained no rationale; the current curriculum remains a compromise between the two traditions of history teaching, with a possible leaning towards the 'alternative' tradition prompted by the introduction of the citizenship curriculum in September 2002. This has further fuelled the debate over the purpose of school history: some history teachers view citizenship as damaging because it is about values education, and overt positions on values can be used to distort rigorous objective history teaching. Others, such as Riley (2000, 2003), believe that objective historical rigour is not the final product but circuitously it takes teachers and students into values.

The issue of teaching the Holocaust in Year 9 and the possible overconcentration on the Nazi period in school history – issues raised in the introduction to this book – may have been averted had the National Curriculum as envisaged by Baker in 1988 not been abandoned. As is shown in Chapters 4 and 5, throughout the development, revision and slimming down of the National Curriculum for History, the Holocaust has gained prominence, ceasing to be an aspect of the Second World War to be taught to Year 10 and 11 students (as it appeared in the final report of the HWG) and emerging as an area of study, for Year 9 students, in its own right. It is a curiosity that a topic currently of such prominence in the National Curriculum for History did not feature in the HWG's interim report. Interviews with members of the Group revealed that Roberts had argued that the Holocaust was important because it changed the demography of eastern Europe and had a catalyst effect on the appearance of Israel; as such, it was important in explaining the Middle East situation. In essence, Roberts believed that a history curriculum for the 21st century should take the long view and incorporate the events and areas of the world that were of such importance that students of secondary age needed an introduction to them. The result was that the two world wars and the Holocaust were not suggested as compulsory topics for study in the HWG's interim report. This decision was reversed, however; Chapter 4 has revealed that there was a lack of clarity regarding why the Holocaust was an important topic for study among those who shaped the National Curriculum for History. Roberts's rationale had been historical; however, it would appear that the two world wars and the Holocaust were included in the HWG's final report for social and moral reasoning and because these events were part of the public consciousness; the omission of these events as named topics of study would, consequently, be too difficult to explain. The debate regarding the Holocaust at the time the National Curriculum was being constructed was about whether or not the topic should be included in the history curriculum rather than discussion of what was important about the Holocaust, what the term 'Holocaust' encompassed and how the Holocaust should be taught in school history. During the two subsequent reviews of the National Curriculum in 1994 and 1999, there was no opportunity to debate and discuss the topic of the Holocaust and how it should be taught in school history. One member of the 1999 History Task Group voiced their amazement at this:

> No discussion of the Holocaust was had on that committee and we were informed by a civil servant that the Holocaust would be compulsory ... I was shocked; this had nothing to do with education. It was not agreed. It was imposed without any guidelines or discussion ... The merits of it were never discussed.
>
> (Interview, 7 January 2003)

A failure to establish the aims and objectives and, therefore, the content and method of history courses on the topic of the Holocaust may go some way to explain the problem identified by Brown and Davies of 'teachers finding it almost impossible to characterize the purpose of the[ir] work clearly' (Brown and Davies 1998: 80).

In so far as teachers are concerned, the importance of theorizing their own practice has not been emphasized: support from government bodies such as the QCA has been practical rather than theoretical. Indeed, Stephen Ball has suggested that the 1988 ERA was the product of a 'profound distrust of teachers', and that one of the aims of the National Curriculum was to reduce teachers to agents of policy which were designed elsewhere (Ball 1990: 171). But it is questionable whether the DfES's control over the curriculum and emphasis on performativity and outcomes has helped to address the deeper causes of 'low standards'. For example, teachers following the QCA scheme of work on the topic of the Holocaust are delivering lessons which have been theorized, debated and designed elsewhere. As a result, teachers may not have themselves considered issues such as whether it is appropriate to discuss the issue of Holocaust denial and how to deal with this question should it arise. Other issues surrounding the use of Anne Frank's story,[2] which is included in the QCA scheme of work, may similarly not have been considered by individual history teachers.

The creation of the National Curriculum could have provided an opportunity to set down for the first time what citizens of the future needed to know about in order to understand the world and their place within it. But, as Chapters 4 and 5 suggest, this was not what the formation of the National Curriculum represented. Ball and Bowe write that, 'it would probably be a generous overstatement to say that the introduction of the National Curriculum is informed by a theory of innovation; clearly it is not' (Ball and Bowe 1992: 106). There was no recognition of the need for a thorough review of curriculum content. MacGregor's letter to Saunders Watson which was published with the HWG's interim report (DES 1989) stressed that the new curriculum should be easy to implement in schools, indicating the absence of a commitment to a thorough review of the school curriculum for the 21st century. The Conservative Government's education reforms were more about gaining greater control over what went on in the classroom.

We need to come to some understanding of what is important about the Holocaust and where on the school curriculum it belongs. The research presented in Chapter 1, albeit small scale, has established that a clear and coherent approach to teaching the Holocaust across the history teaching profession is lacking: history teachers' motivations for teaching the Holocaust are varied, as is the amount of time spent teaching the Holocaust.

It is difficult to establish a direct link between a lack of clarity regarding the rationale behind the inclusion of the Holocaust among those who have shaped the National Curriculum for History and the variety of motives that surround the teaching of the topic in the Key Stage 3 history classroom. Yet it is clear that the debate surrounding how the Holocaust should be understood and presented in history lessons is complex, and it seems the lack of a rationale contributes to the wide variety of ways in which the topic of the Holocaust is approached by history teachers.

This lack of rationale raised questions in my mind regarding the impact of this on classroom practice: had the National Curriculum not been introduced, perhaps the teaching of the Holocaust would have become widespread in schools, building on the pioneering work of the ILEA. The introduction of the National Curriculum meant that history teachers *had* to teach the Holocaust. The question of why history teachers *should* teach the Holocaust, a question that Clive Lawton had identified as being of primary importance in his 1985 lecture (ILEA 1985), appears to have been sidelined. However, in Chapter 1 it was highlighted that despite being a compulsory topic in the National Curriculum for History, the Holocaust is not taught to all school students: teachers need to be convinced of the importance of teaching the Holocaust. The questions of what is important about the

Holocaust and why it was included in the National Curriculum for History are of continued relevance and have implications for teaching and learning.

This study was motivated in large part by my own lack of opportunity to theorize the teaching of the Holocaust in school history while in the classroom. Fernandez-Armesto (2002) has commented that in recent years school history has been neglected by historians who have been distracted by changes in the nature of historical study. Academic historians may have a role to play in supporting the professional development of history teachers. There are also implications in terms of school structures. In Chapter 1, teachers lamented their lack of time to read and keep abreast of debates in school history. Teachers require fewer administrative pressures on their time, distracting them from reading and reflecting on their teaching. Debates about the uniqueness of the Holocaust, the purpose of school history and how far moral issues should come into the teaching of the Holocaust in school history are likely to continue. What is important is that ordinary history teachers have ownership of these debates and the opportunity to theorize their practice.

Notes

Introduction

1. The Education Reform Act, passed in 1988, heralded the development of a National Curriculum for England and Wales. Kenneth Baker, who was the Secretary of State for Education at the time, announced proposals for a 'national core curriculum' on London Weekend Television's *Weekend World*, broadcast on 7 December 1986. There followed in 1987 an Education Reform Bill upon which the Education Reform Act was based (Chitty 2002). This Act provided for the establishment of a national curriculum of core (maths, science, English) and foundation (technology, history, geography, modern foreign languages, art, music, physical education) subjects. For each subject there were objectives, known as attainment targets, for the knowledge, skills and understanding that students should be expected to have acquired by the end of the academic year in which they were aged 7, 11, 14 and 16. These were 'key ages' and therefore students aged between 5 and 7 were in Key Stage 1, students aged 7 to 11 were in Key Stage 2, students aged 11 to 14 were in Key Stage 3 and those aged 14 to16 were in Key Stage 4. Programmes of study were to be drawn up to detail the content, skills and processes that would need to be covered during each key stage. The attainment targets and programmes of study would together form the basis of the Standard Attainment Tasks (SATs) which would assess students at the end of each key stage. Subject-based working groups were established to develop the attainment targets and programmes of study for each National Curriculum subject. In 1991, the National Curriculum, drawn up by these subject working groups and approved by the Government, became statutory.
2. See <http://www.bbc.co.uk/print/pressoffice/pressreleases/stories/2004/12_december/02/auschwitz.shtml>.
3. 'Shoah' is Hebrew for 'a great and terrible wind'. It is a term preferred by some in place of 'Holocaust'.
4. As noted, there is a policy of selection in Kent. Therefore, while this school called itself a comprehensive, it could not be described as being fully comprehensive.
5. One member of the HWG has died since this work was begun. John Roberts died on 30 May 2003.

1 History teachers on teaching the Holocaust

1. It should be noted that Hank's comments are possibly evidence of a lack of familiarity with the National Curriculum since the Holocaust is a compulsory part of the history curriculum.

2 What was the Holocaust?

1. See lower on p. 47 for a definition of T4.
2. The term 'Holocaust education' also appears in this book to describe teaching about the Holocaust, the events which led up to it and the moral and social lessons drawn from the Holocaust. However, not all those in the field support the use of this term to describe the teaching of social and moral lessons arising from the Holocaust. The American writer Sam Totten (1999) sees that lessons which, for example, involve classroom discussion of universal themes such as tolerance (where the Holocaust is used as the starting point for discussion) should be more accurately referred to as 'prejudice reduction' or 'human-rights awareness'. Short, in response to Totten's view that 'Holocaust education is a misnomer when used to refer to anything other than the genocide itself and events leading up to it', has written that Totten's emphasis on terminology is misplaced and that 'the priority is not to challenge the legitimacy of the term' (Short 2003a: 121). Although it could be argued that, strictly speaking, Totten is correct, the term is generally accepted and commonly used to describe teaching about the Holocaust and the events which led up to it as well as lessons that can be drawn from the Holocaust concerned with human rights.
3. In April 1993, President Clinton opened the Holocaust Memorial Museum in New York with the words 'Never Again'. Paris notes the irony of this statement given that Bosnian civilians were being killed at the time (Paris 2002: 336).
4. In fact, research published by Laurence Rees in his 2005 book *Auschwitz: the Nazis and the Final Solution* suggests that the motivation behind the introduction of the gas chambers was not about speed but finding an 'effective way of killing people that minimized the psychological impact of the crime on the killers'. Heinrich Himmler became aware that men in his killing squads were experiencing psychological problems and becoming brutalized after he visited Minsk in August 1941 and witnessed their work (Rees 2005: 68–70).
5. That said, the Holocaust was never inevitable. It is important for students to understand Christian anti-Judaism but not see it as a prime cause of the Holocaust. It would be a mistake to say that the Holocaust is a result of Christian anti-Judaism; that tradition could have continued, or been overcome, without it ever coming to the Holocaust.

3   Teaching the Holocaust before 1991

1. This video also contained *Talking to Survivors*, a 30-minute programme in which students from four schools in London (Hampstead School, Pimlico School, Tower Hamlets School and Tulse Hill School) put questions to Holocaust survivors Rabbi Hugo Gryn, Marsha Segall and Ben Helfgott. Ben Helfgott was a member of the 45 Aid Society, a charitable organization made up of a group of 732 Holocaust survivors who came to Britain after the war in 1945. Most of them were in their late teens. They travelled under the sponsorship of the Central British Fund, a Jewish organization which had been active in helping refugees since the rise of Hitler in 1933. Most of them were boys – about 80 were girls. Sir Martin Gilbert has written a book detailing the experiences of this group (Gilbert 1996). Members of the 45 Aid Society began giving regular talks in the 1980s about their experiences to school students. On 12 June 1989, the *Jewish Chronicle* reported on a talk given by Helfgott to students at a girls' school in north London.

2. GCHQ stands for Government Communications Headquarters. GCHQ is the government department responsible for monitoring intelligence relevant to the UK. In 1984, Thatcher's Conservative Government banned trade-union membership among its employees at GCHQ. There was a strong reaction to this policy and it was not repeated elsewhere in other government departments.

3. Political pressure forced the ILEA to withdraw its teaching materials on the Holocaust. The ILEA was disbanded in 1990.

4. Yad Vashem, the Holocaust Martyrs' and Heroes' Remembrance Authority was established in 1953 to commemorate the 6 million Jews murdered by the Nazis and their collaborators. Yad Vashem is situated on Har Hazikaron, the Mount of Remembrance, and extends over 45 acres on which there are two museums, exhibition halls, outdoor monuments and major archives.

5. The members of this committee were Ben Helfgott, Antony Polonsky, John Fox, Shirley Murgraff and Ronnie Landau.

6. Further additions to the Trust's board were noted in this correspondence. Ivan Lawrence, described as a Conservative, member of the Board of Deputies and a close friend of Janner, was to be the Trust's Secretary. It was hoped Elizabeth Maxwell would agree to become a trustee, and the Revd Leslie Hardman, whom Janner noted had been Chaplain to the British Forces when they entered Belsen, had joined the Board of Management.

7. The Spiro Institute, now called the London Jewish Cultural Centre, is an organization that has taught Jewish history, culture and Modern Hebrew for over 20 years.

8. Kenneth Baker was Secretary of State for Education from May 1986 until July 1989.

9. This term has been defined by Chitty (1989) as a collection of educationalists, philosophers and economists who influenced successive Secretaries of State for Education and Prime Ministers. The New Right encompassed various right-wing groups such as the Hillgate Group which began publishing campaigning pamphlets at the end of 1986.

10. Cheryl Bailey took over from Phil Snell in August 1989.

11. Prochaska wrote in the *History Workshop Journal* of her experiences as a member of the History Working Group in which she commented,

> you are only given the chance to say yes or no, not to put forward more suitable people. So someone even less suitable may well take your place if you say no. Then, since the legislation is in being and the National Curriculum will come about regardless of individuals' scruples, the opportunity to help make it as good as possible is not to be turned down. (Prochaska 1990: 81–2)

4 The question of whether the Holocaust should be compulsory in school history

1. All those interviewed recalled the following discussion took place after dinner at Hebden Bridge. Present at the Hebden Bridge meeting were Michael Saunders Watson, Robert Guyver, Jim Hendy, Gareth Elwyn Jones, Tom Hobhouse, Peter Livsey, Ann Low-Beer, John Roberts (arrived on 31 May) and Carol White. Also in attendance were Michael Phipps (DES) and Roger Hennessey (HMI Observer) as well as the Secretariat Jenny Worsfold, Phil Snell and Lesley Storey. Alice Prochaska was unable to attend this meeting.

2. These were the motivations cited by John Roberts in a letter to myself, 14 May 2002.

3. The HWG viewed the Holocaust as part of the Nazi period and never discussed it as a topic in its own right, separate from the Second World War.

4. In fact, Roberts had handed a letter of resignation to Saunders Watson at Hebden Bridge. He was unable to balance his commitments as Warden of Merton College Oxford and a high-profile historian with sitting on the Group. Given what he considered his poor record of attendance, he decided to resign following the publication of the interim report. He had missed five out of nine meetings. Roberts was replaced by Professor Peter Marshall.

5. Interview, 20 June 2002, supported by comments made during an interview with the Chairperson, 11 July 2002.

6. As detailed in the chronology, this group was set up by Saunders Watson during the HWG's 13th meeting (30 August–1 September) to deal with the responses the Group received to its interim report. At the same meeting, two other panels were set up by the Chairperson to deal with the tasks ahead: the Programmes of Study Panel and the Assessment Panel. The names of those members who served on each panel are listed in the chronology.

7. The final three on this list were the Reformation/the history of Christianity, the 'history of medicine', more European history generally.

8. A Conservative MP who had pressured the British Government to open its files on Austrian President Kurt Waldheim to investigate his relationship with the Nazis.

9. A Labour MP who had campaigned for SS Maj.-Gen. Wilhelm Mohnke to be tried for the murder of British prisoners near Dunkirk in 1940.

10. Letter from Greville Janner, John Marshall, Robert Rhodes James and Jeff Rooker, 29 September 1989.

11. This was recalled in an interview with the HMI Observer, 20 June 2002 as well as the Chairperson, 11 July 2002.

12. One of the 'what ifs' of history is whether if Roberts had remained on the HWG the decision to include the Second World War as a mandatory programme of study in the final report would have been so easy for the Group. Members of the HWG mentioned in interview that they felt it would have been difficult to reverse the Hebden Bridge decision had Roberts continued to sit on the Group. Comments from leading group members included 'There may have been some arguments if John Roberts had stayed' (interview, 24 June 2002) and 'If he had remained on the group I think we would have had a hard time getting out of that' (interview, 11 July 2002).

13. Unhappy with the content of the final report, Thatcher delayed its publication and insisted that the Secretary of State put the proposals out for further consultation. The report was published on 3 April 1990.

5   Teaching the Holocaust in school history since 1991

1. Much of the work of the SCAA Advisory Group for History was concentrated not upon curriculum content but upon establishing the second-order concepts which became the key elements in the 1995 National Curriculum for History.

2. In 1997, the SCAA was merged with the National Council for Vocational Qualifications (NCVQ) to form the QCA.

3. Teaching about European History and Society in the 1990s, Tuusula (Finland) August 1991.

4. Schemes are also available for Key Stage 1 and 2.

5. The two world wars and the Cold War do not each have their own QCA scheme of work but are covered by Unit 18 'Hot War, Cold War: why did the major twentieth-century conflicts affect so many people?' This unit, expected to be taught over 10–15 hours, is described by the QCA as follows:

    In this unit pupils learn about the main conflicts of the twentieth century by identifying key ideas and themes and making links and connections, particularly between the First World War, the Second World War and the Cold War. The unit focuses on the widespread impact of these conflicts through the examination of specific events, the personal experiences of individuals and a wide range of visual and written sources.

    (<http://www.standards.dfes.gov.uk/schemes2/secondary_history/his18/?view=
    get>)

6. Peter Novick is an historian and has written *The Holocaust in American Life* in which he says he finds the idea of students learning social and moral lessons from the Holocaust 'dubious' (Novick 1999).

7. Short writes that Jews and Muslims:

> are equally vulnerable to the threat posed by indigenous neo-Nazi movements. The nature of that threat, as far as Muslims are concerned, can be appreciated by studying Hitler's rise to power, as it is clear that the Nazis were ideologically (though not politically) dismissive of the Arabs. Alfred Rosenberg, for example, the Nazis' key racial theorist warned the white peoples of Europe to be on their guard 'against the united hatreds of coloured races and mongrels, led in the fanatical spirit of Mohammed'.
> (Short 1998: 12)

Short goes on to suggest that teaching the Holocaust 'might help Jews and other ethnic minorities to make common cause in the wider struggle against racism' (Short 1998: 13). It would be interesting to research whether and how widely the Holocaust is discussed in schools with Jewish and Muslim students from this perspective.

Conclusion

1. The QCA could not locate drafts of this scheme of work within their archives or confirm or deny that Holocaust denial had been an element of work suggested in a draft of their scheme of work on the Holocaust.

2. Anne Frank's experience was exceptional; her story does not portray the common experience, and on this basis there are questions regarding whether it is the best resource to use with students learning about the Holocaust.

Bibliography

Ahonen, S. (2001) Politics of Identity through History Curiculum: narratives of the past for social exclusion – or inclusion? *Journal of Curriculum Studies*, 33(2): 179–94.

Arthur, J. (2000) What are the issues in the teaching of history? In J. Arthur and R. Phillips (eds), *Issues in History Teaching*. London: Routledge, pp. 1–9.

Arthur, J., and Wright, D. (eds) (2001) *Teaching Citizenship in the Secondary School*. London: David Fulton.

Ascherson, N. (2003) Still spellbound by the Nazis. *The Observer Review*. 30 November, p. 15.

Baker, K. (1993) *The Turbulent Years: my life in politics*. London: Faber and Faber.

Ball, S. (1990) *Politics and Policy Making in Education: explorations in policy sociology*. London: Routledge.

Ball, S. and Bowe, R. (1992) Subject Departments and the 'Implementation' of National Curriculum Policy: an overview of the issues. *Journal of Curriculum Studies*, 24(2): 97–115.

Bauman, Z. (1989) *Modernity and the Holocaust*. Ithaca, NY: Cornell University Press.

Beattie, A. (1987) *History in Peril: may parents preserve it*. London: Centre for Policy Studies.

Blum, P. (1990) Past Perfect and Present Imperfect. *AMMA*, 12(3): 10–11.

Blumenthal, M. W. (2001) Welcome to the Jewish Museum Berlin. In *Stories of an Exhibition*. Berlin: Stiftung Judisches Museum Berlin, pp. 14–17.

Bresheeth, H., Hood, S. and Jansz, L. (2000) *Introducing the Holocaust*. Cambridge: Icon Books.

Brown, M. and Davies, I. (1988) The Holocaust and Education for Citizenship: the teaching of history, religion and human rights in England. *Educational Review*, 50(1): 75–83.

Byrom, J. and Riley, M. (2003) Professional Wrestling in the History Department: a case study in planning the teaching of the British Empire at Key Stage 3. *Teaching History*, 112.

Carr, E. H. (1961) *What is History?* London: Macmillan.

Chitty, C. (2002) *Understanding Schools and Schooling*. London: RoutledgeFalmer.

Coltham, J. and Fines, J. (1971) *Educational Objectives for the Study of History*. London: Historical Association.

Counsell, C. (2002a) Editorial. *Teaching History*, 109, 2.

—— (2002b) Editorial. *Teaching History*, 106, 2.

—— (2002c) *History for All. Past Forward: a vision for school history 2002–2012*. London: The Historical Association.

Counsell, C. and Kinloch, N. (2001) Editorial. *Teaching History*, 104, 2.

Crace, J. (2002) Always remember. *Guardian Education*, 19 November, pp. 4–5.

Crawford, K. (1995) A History of the Right: the battle for control of National Curriculum History 1989–1994. *British Journal of Educational Studies* (4): 433–456.

Davies, I. (ed.) (2000) *Teaching the Holocaust: educational dimensions, principles and practice*. London: Continuum.

Department of Education and Science (DES) (1988) *Curriculum Matters 5–16: History*. London: HMSO.

—— (1989) *National Curriculum History Working Group: Interim Report*. London: HMSO.

—— (1990) *National Curriculum History Working Group: Final Report*. London: HMSO.

—— (1991a) *History in the National Curriculum (England)*. London: HMSO.

—— (14 January 1991b) *7/91*. London: HMSO.

Department for Education (DfE) (1995) *History in the National Curriculum: England*. London: HMSO.

Department for Education and Employment (DfEE) (1999) *History: The National Curriculum for England*. London: HMSO.

Drescher, S. (1996) The Atlantic Slave Trade and the Holocaust: a comparative analysis. In A. S. Rosenbaum (ed.) *Is the Holocaust Unique? Perspectives on comparative genocide*. Oxford: Westview Press, pp. 65–86.

Elton, G. R. (1967) *The Practice of History*. London: Methuen.

Evans, R. J. (1997) *In Defence of History*. London: Granta Books.

—— (2003) *The Coming of the Third Reich*. London: Allen Lane.

Fawcett, G. (2001) Teaching History and the German Right. *History Today*, 16–17.

Fernandez-Armesto, F. (2002) What is History *Now*? In D. Cannadine (ed.) *What is History Now?* Basingstoke: PalgraveMacmillan, pp. 148–61.

Finch, J. (1986) *Research and Policy: the use of qualitative methods in social and educational research*. London: Falmer Press.

Fitz, J. and Halpin, D. (1994) Ministers and Mandarins: educational research in elite settings. In G. Walford (ed.) *Researching the Powerful in Education*. London: UCL Press, pp. 32–50.

Fox, J. P. (1989) *Teaching the Holocaust: the report of a survey in the United Kingdom (1987)*: The National Yad Vashem Charitable Trust and the Centre for Holocaust Studies, University of Leicester.

—— (2001) Holocaust Education in Europe. In W. Laqueur (ed.) *The Holocaust Encyclopedia*. New Haven, Conn. and London: Yale University Press, pp. 301–5.

Freeman, J. (2002) New Opportunities for History: implementing the citizenship curriculum in England's secondary schools – a QCA perspective. *Teaching History*, 106: 28–32.

Gilbert, M. (1996) *The Boys: triumph over adversity*. London: Weidenfeld & Nicolson.

Glanz, J. (2001) *Holocaust Handbook for Teachers: materials and strategies for Grades 5–12*. Dubuque, Iowa: Kendall/Hunt Publishers.

Glass, J. (1997) *'Life Unworthy of Life': Racial Phobia and Mass Murder in Hitler's Germany*. New York: Basic Books.

Godsell, C. (2001) They Came to History . . . *Teaching History*, 105, 5.

Gourevitch, P. (1999) *We Wish to Inform You that Tomorrow We Will Be Killed with Our Families*. London: Macmillan.

Granath, A. (2002) A brighter past. *TES Teacher*, 14 June, pp. 24–5.

Gregory, I. (2000a) The Holocaust: Some Reflections and Issues. In I. Davies (ed.) *Teaching the Holocaust: educational dimensions, principles and practice*. London: Continuum, pp. 37–47.

—— (2000b) Teaching about the Holocaust: perplexities, issues and suggestions. In I. Davies (ed.) *Teaching the Holocaust: educational dimensions, principles and practice*. London: Continuum, pp. 49–60.

Griffiths, R. (1983) *Fellow Travellers of the Right: British enthusiasts for Nazi Germany, 1933–1939*. Oxford: Oxford University Press.

Guyver, R. (1990) History's Domesday Book. *History Workshop Journal* (30): 100–8.

Hammond, K. (2001) From Horror to History: teaching pupils to reflect on significance. *Teaching History*, 104, 15–23.

Haydn, T. (2000) Teaching the Holocaust through History. In I. Davies (ed.) *Teaching the Holocaust: educational dimensions, principles and practice*. London: Continuum, pp. 135–49.

Haydn, T., Arthur, J. and Hunt, M. (1997) *Learning to Teach History in the Secondary School*. London: Routledge.

Hector, S. (2000) Teaching the Holocaust in England. In I. Davies (ed.) *Teaching the Holocaust: educational dimensions, principles and practice*. London: Continuum, pp. 105–15.

—— (2003) *The Holocaust in Secondary Classrooms: a comparison between the attitudes and choices of history teachers and religious education teachers*. Unpublished manuscript, School of Education, Westminster College, Oxford.

Hennessey, R. (1988) The School History Question. *The Historian*.

Hobhouse, H. (1989) *The Forces of Change: why we are the way we are now*. London: Sidgwick & Jackson.

Hunter, A. (1993) Local Knowledge and Local Power: notes on the ethnography of local community elites. *Journal of Contemporary Ethnography*, 22: 36–58.

Husbands, C., Kitson, A. and Pendry, A. (2003) *Understanding History Teaching: teaching and learning about the past in secondary schools*. Maidenhead and Philadelphia, Pa.: Open University Press.

Illingworth, S. (2000) Hearts, Minds and Souls: exploring values through history. *Teaching History*, 100: 20–24.

Inner London Education Authority (ILEA) (1985) Teaching the Holocaust: a lecture by Clive Lawton. London: Inner London Education Authority Learning Materials Service.

Jones, G. E. (1991) Making History: a personal view of History in the National Curriculum. *Welsh Journal of Education*, 3 (1): 3–9.

Katz, S. T. (1994) *The Holocaust in Historical Context: Volume 1*. New York: Oxford University Press.

—— (1996) The Uniqueness of the Holocaust: the historical dimension. In A. S. Rosenbaum (ed.) *Is the Holocaust Unique? Perspectives on comparative genocide*. Oxford: Westview.

Kedourie, E. (1984) *The Crossman Confessions and Other Essays in Politics, History and Religion*. London: Mansel.

King, D. (1999) *In the Name of Liberalism: illiberal social policy in the United States and Britain.* Oxford: Oxford University Press.

Kinloch, N. (1998) Learning about the Holocaust: moral or historical question? *Teaching History*, 93: 44–6.

—— (2001) Parallel catastrophes? Uniqueness, redemption and the Shoah. *Teaching History* (8): 8–14.

Klein, R. (1992) Facing Up to the Final Solution. *The Times Educational Supplement*, 17 April, pp. 31–2.

Lambert, D. (2004) Geography in the Holocaust: citizenship denied. *Teaching History*, 116: 42–8.

Lang, S. (1999) Democracy is NOT boring. *Teaching History* (96) 23–7.

Lawton, D., and Chitty, C. (eds) (1988) *The National Curriculum.* London: Institute of Education.

Lipstadt, D. (1994) *Denying the Holocaust: the growing assault on truth and memory.* London: Penguin.

Longworth, N. (1981) We're Moving into the Information Society – what shall we tell the children? *Computer Education* (June) 17–19.

Lopate, P. (1989) Resistance to the Holocaust. In D. Rosenberg (ed.) *Testimony: contemporary writers make the Holocaust personal.* New York: Times Books.

Low-Beer, A. (1967) Moral Judgments in History and History Teaching. In H. Burston and D. Thompson (eds) *Studies in the Nature and Teaching of History*, London: Routledge & Kegan Paul, pp. 137–58.

—— (1987) Feeling doubtful. *The Times Educational Supplement*, 10 April.

—— (1988) Examining Feelings. *World Studies Journal*, 7(2).

—— (1989) Empathy and History. *Teaching History*, 8–12.

Maitles, H. and Cowan, P. (1999) Teaching the Holocaust in Primary Schools in Scotland: modes, methodology and content. *Educational Review*, 51 (3): 263–71.

Marrus, M. R. (1987) *The Holocaust in History.* Hanover: Brandeis University Press and University Press of New England.

Marshall, G. (1999) Letter. *Teaching History*, 95, 3.

McLaughlin, T. (1999) Letter. *Teaching History*, 96, 3.

Meagher, M. (1999) Letter. *Teaching History*, 94, 3.

Melson, R. F. (1996) The American Genocide as Precursor and Prototype of Twentieth-Century Genocide. In A. S. Rosenbaum (ed.) *Is the Holocaust Unique? Perspectives on comparative genocide.* Oxford: Westview Press.

Malvern, L. R. (2000) *A People Betrayed: the role of the West in Rwanda's genocide.* London and New York: Zed Books.

Milton, M. (1976) *Never to Forget: the Jews of the Holocaust.* New York: HarperCollins.

Moloney, A. (2003). Learning issue. *Jewish Chronicle*, 12 September, p. 33.

Mountford, P. (2001) Working as a Team to Teach the Holocaust Well: a language-centred approach. *Teaching History*, 104: 28–33.

Mullan, J. (2005) The Meaning of Holocaust. *The Guardian*, 25 January, p. 4.

Nash, I. (1991) When History Ends, Current Affairs Begin. *The Times Educational Supplement*, 18 January.

NCC and SEAC defs. (1993) *The National Curriculum and its Assessment: an interim report.* York, NCC; London, SEAC.

Niven, B. (2002) *Facing the Nazi Past.* London and New York: Routledge.

Novick, P. (1999) *The Holocaust in American Life.* New York: Houghton Mifflin.

Ostrander, S. (1993) 'Surely you're not in this just to be helpful?' Access, rapport, and interviews in three studies of elites. *Journal of Contemporary Ethnography,* 22: 7–27.

Oz, A. (1988) The Meaning of Homeland. *New Outlook,* 31 (1): 19–24.

Paris, E. (2002) *Long Shadows: truth, lies and history.* London: Bloomsbury.

Phillips, M. (1996) *All Must Have Prizes.* London: Little, Brown & Company.

Phillips, R. (1998) *History Teaching, Nationhood and the State.* London: Cassell.

—— (2002) *Reflective Teaching of History 11–18.* London: Continuum.

Phillips, R., Goalen, P., McNully, A. and Wood, S. (1999) Four Histories, One Nation? History teaching, nationhood and a British identity. *Compare,* 29 (2): 153–69.

Plowright, J. (1991) Teaching the Holocaust: a response to the report on a United Kingdom Survey. *Teaching History,* 62: 26–29.

Price, M. (1968) History in Danger. *History,* 53: 342–7.

Prochaska, S. (1982) *History of the General Federation of Trade Unions 1899–1980.* London: Allen & Unwin.

—— (1990) The History Working Group: reflections and diary. *History Workshop Journal* (30): 80–90.

Qualifications and Curriculum Authority (QCA) (1998) *Education for Citizenship and the Teaching of Democracy in Schools: final report of the Advisory Group on Citizenship 22 September 1998.* London: Qualifications and Curriculum Authority.

—— (2000) *Key stage 3 Schemes of Work: Unit 19 How and why did the Holocaust happen?* London: Qualifications and Curriculum Authority.

Raab, C. (1987) Oral History as an Instrument of Research into Scottish Educational Policy-Making. In G. Moyser and M. Wagstaffe (eds) *Research Methods for Elite Studies.* London: Allen & Unwin.

Rees, L. (2005) *Auschwitz the Nazis and the 'Final Solution'.* London: BBC Books.

Rees Jones, S. (2000) The Roots of Antisemitism. In I. Davies (ed.) *Teaching the Holocaust: Educational Dimensions, Principles and Practice.* London: Continuum, pp. 11–23.

Reynoldson, F. (1993) *The Era of the 2nd World War: foundation history.* Oxford: Heinemann Educational.

Richards, H. (2003) Time to Make Nazis History, or Is There Life in Hitler Yet? *Times Higher Education Supplement,* 23 January.

Riley, M. (2000) Into the Key Stage 3 History Garden: choosing and planting your enquiry questions. *Teaching History,* 99.

Rogers, P. J. (1984) Why Teach History? In K. Dickinson A. P. J. Lee and P. J. Rogers (eds) *Learning History.* London: Heinemann Educational Books, pp. 20–38.

Rosenbaum, A. S. (ed.) (1996) *Is the Holocaust Unique? Perspectives on comparative genocide.* Oxford: Westview Press.

Rowbotham, S. (1973) *Hidden from History: 300 years of women's oppression and the fight against it.* London: Pluto Press.

Russell, L. (2001) Letter. *Teaching History,* 105: 3.

—— (2002) The Wider Picture, *Times Educational Supplement Teacher*, 14 June: 27.

Said, E. (1993) *Culture and Imperialism*. London: Chatto & Windus.

Salmons, P. (2001) Moral Dilemmas: history, teaching and the Holocaust. *Teaching History*, 104: 34–40.

Seldon, A. and Pappworth, J. (1983) *By Word of Mouth: elite oral history*. London: Methuen.

Short, G. (1995) The Holocaust in the National Curriculum: a survey of teachers' attitudes and practices. *Journal of Holocaust Education*, 4: 167–88.

—— (1998) Teaching the Holocaust. In G. Short, C. Supple and K. Klinger (eds) *The Holocaust in the School Curriculum: a European perspective*. Germany: Council of Europe.

—— (2003a) Holocaust Education in the Primary School. *London Review of Education*, 1 (2): 119–29.

—— (2003b) Lessons of the Holocaust: a response to the critics. *Educational Review*, 55 (3): 277–87.

Slater, J. (1995) *Teaching History in the New Europe*. London: Cassell.

Stannard, D. (1996) The Politics of Genocide Scholarship. In A. S. Rosenbaum (ed.) *Is The Holocaust Unique? Perspectives on comparative genocide*. Oxford: Westview.

Stead, G. (1986) Holocaust Lessons for Britain Today. *Jewish Chronicle*, 28 March, p. 26.

Stradling, R. (2001) *Teaching 20th-century European History*. Strasbourg: Council of Europe.

Supple, C. (1992) *The Teaching of the Nazi Holocaust in North Tyneside, Newcastle and Northumberland Secondary Schools*. Unpublished MS, School of Education, Newcastle upon Tyne.

—— (1998) Issues and Problems in Teaching about the Holocaust. In *The Holocaust in the School Curriculum: a European perspective*. Strasbourg: Council of Europe.

Teaching about the Holocaust: A resource book for educators (2001) Washington, DC: The United States Memorial Museum.

Thatcher, M. (1993) *The Downing Street Years*. London: HarperCollins.

Thompson, E. P. (1965) *The Making of the English Working Class*. Harmondsworth: Penguin.

Tosh, J. (1991) *The Pursuit of History: aims, methods and new directions in the study of modern history*, 2nd edn. London: Longman.

Totten, S. (1999) Should There Be Holocaust Education for K-4 Students? The answer is no. *Social Studies and the Young Learner*, 12: 36–39.

Wasserstein, B. (1979) *Britain and the Jews of Europe, 1939–1945*. Oxford: Oxford University Press.

Wiesel, E. (1988) Some Questions that Remain Open. In A. Cohen, J. Gelber and C. Wardi (eds) *Comprehending the Holocaust*. Frankfurt: Peter Lang.

Wrenn, A. (1999) Build It In, Don't Bolt It On: history's opportunity to support critical citizenship. *Teaching History*, 96: 6–12.

Index